Parental Vigilant Care

This volume presents the concept of vigilant care as a protective and non-intrusive parental attitude to risky behaviors of children and adolescents. The effective component in vigilant care is not control, but parental presence. Vigilant care is a flexible attitude in which parents shift between levels of open attention, focused attention, and protective action, according to the alarm signals they detect. The author presents a detailed theoretical, empirical, and clinical rationale for the model, which deals with potentially problematic parental attitudes or parent–child processes such as overparenting, psychological control, disregard of legitimate personal domains or of the child's need for self-determination, parent–child mutual distancing, and escalation.

Haim Omer, PhD, is Professor in the School of Psychological Sciences at Tel Aviv University, and is the founder and professional director of the Parent-Training Center at the Schneider Children's Hospital in Petah Tivka, Israel. He is the author of several books and is the developer of "non-violent resistance" as a therapeutic approach to violent, risk-taking, and self-destructive children and adolescents.

Parental Vigilant Care
A Guide for Clinicians and Caretakers

Haim Omer

NEW YORK AND LONDON

First published 2017
by Routledge
711 Third Avenue, New York, NY 10017

and by Routledge
2 Park Square, Milton Park, Abingdon, Oxon, OX14 4RN

Routledge is an imprint of the Taylor & Francis Group, an informa business

© 2017 Taylor & Francis

The right of Haim Omer to be identified as the author of this work in accordance with sections 77 and 78 of the Copyright, Designs and Patents Act 1988.

All rights reserved. No part of this book may be reprinted or reproduced or utilised in any form or by any electronic, mechanical, or other means, now known or hereafter invented, including photocopying and recording, or in any information storage or retrieval system, without permission in writing from the publishers.

Trademark notice: Product or corporate names may be trademarks or registered trademarks, and are used only for identification and explanation without intent to infringe.

Library of Congress Cataloging-in-Publication Data
A catalog record for this book has been requested

ISBN: 978-1-138-65104-3 (hbk)
ISBN: 978-1-138-65105-0 (pbk)
ISBN: 978-1-315-62497-6 (ebk)

Typeset in Baskerville
by Deanta Global Publishing Services, Chennai, India

Contents

1. Vigilant Care — 1
   WITH OREN DRITTER AND SHAI SATRAN

2. Vigilant Care in Daily Life — 31
   WITH TAL FISHER AND SHAI SATRAN

3. When the Child Resists — 46
   WITH YOEL EVERETT

4. Lies — 62
   WITH SHAI SATRAN

5. Friends — 73
   WITH GABRIELA HANGA

6. Money — 86
   WITH YAEL NEVAT AND TAL FISHER

7. Cigarettes, Alcohol and Drugs — 98
   WITH TAL CARTY, DAN SOLOMON AND AVIGAIL HIRSCH-ASA

8. Computers and the Internet — 108
   WITH YARON SELA

9. Diabetes — 118
   WITH YAEL ROTHMAN-KABIR

10. Vigilant Care Among Juvenile Offenders — 124
    HAIM OMER AND ZOHAR LOTRINGER IN COLLABORATION WITH
    THE ISRAELI JUVENILE PROBATION SERVICE AND THE OR YAROK
    ASSOCIATION FOR PREVENTION OF ROAD ACCIDENTS

11	Teen Driving WITH C. T. JURAVEL AND Y. SHIMSHONI	130
	Conclusion	138
	List of contributors	140
	Index	141

1 Vigilant Care

with Oren Dritter and Shai Satran

Parents are often confused when it comes to what is the best attitude regarding the prevention of risk behaviors by children, and especially by adolescents. On the one hand, they want to monitor their children closely, so as to know about any danger or temptation to which the child may be exposed. On the other hand, they want to develop an atmosphere of trust that may encourage their children to confide in them spontaneously. Both aims are worthy, but at times they are bound to clash, putting the parents in a difficult dilemma. Thus, in trying to promote openness and trust, the parents may find out that their child has lied to them or is involved in problematic friendships or activities; or in trying to supervise their child's activities closely, the parents may find out that the relationship deteriorates, that the child fights back or blames them, sometimes rightfully, for impinging on her[1] autonomy and damaging her social life. Interestingly, research on parenting and risk prevention seems to be affected by the same dilemma: some authorities in the field adduce evidence that spontaneous disclosure by the child is the key to risk prevention, and that unilateral parental supervision might not only be unhelpful, but even detrimental to the atmosphere that is conducive to disclosure (Kerr et al., 2010); others adduce no less convincing evidence that, without decided parental supervision, adolescents exposed to risk situations may fare badly (Keijsers et al., 2009; Keijsers & Laird, 2014; Soenens et al., 2006). The purpose of this book is to present a comprehensive model of *vigilant care* that may help solve this dilemma.

Scientific opinion on this matter has not always been thus divided. Most theorists and researchers once considered *parental monitoring* the gold standard for increasing the safety of children and adolescents regarding a wide variety of risk factors. Dishion and McMahon (1998) characterized parental monitoring as "a set of correlated parenting behaviors involving attention to and tracking of the child's whereabouts, activities and adaptations" (p. 61). Over the years, an abundance of research accumulated, resulting in massive empirical support linking monitoring to risk reduction. This bulk of evidence seemed to offer a clear and simple message to parents: "Monitor your child!" Studies linking increased parental monitoring with reduced danger cover virtually all fields of child and adolescent risk behaviors, such as substance abuse (Beck, Boyle &

Boekeloo, 2004; Ensminger, Juon & Fothergill, 2002; Wood, Read, Mitchell & Brand, 2004), negative peer group association (Dishion, Nelson & Bullock, 2004; Rodgers-Farmer, 2001), violent and delinquent behavior (Chamberlain & Reid, 1998; Cookston, 1999; Jacobson & Crockett, 2000; Laird, Pettit, Bates & Dodge, 2003; Wright & Cullen, 2001), gambling (Magoon & Ingersoll, 2006), early and unsafe sex, venereal diseases and early pregnancy (Cohen, Farley, Taylor, Martin & Schuster, 2002; DiClemente et al., 2001; Rai et al., 2003; Wilder & Watt, 2002), scholastic problems (Crouter, MacDermid, McHale & Perry-Jenkins, 1990; Plunkett & Bamaca-Gomez, 2003; Toney, Kelley & Lanclos, 2003), teen cigarette smoking (Dalton et al., 2006; Rai et al., 2003), computer misuse (Sorbring & Lundin, 2012; Steeves & Webster, 2007) and unsafe driving (Bingham & Shope, 2004; Hartos, Eitel, Haynie & Simons-Morton, 2000; Hartos, Eitel & Simmons-Morton, 2002). Research has shown that monitoring prevents risk both with boys and girls (Crouter et al., 1990; Jacobson & Crockett, 2000; Kilgore, Snyder & Lentz, 2000), and with families of various cultural, ethnic and socio-economic backgrounds (Li et al., 2000; Ramirez et al., 2004).

The assumption underlying most of this research is that the relationship between parental monitoring and risk is linear: the more monitoring, the less risk. Considerable evidence, however, suggests that differences in the intensity, kind and context of monitoring, as well as in family atmosphere, child characteristics and age, can lead to very different results, subverting the assumption of linearity. Criticism of the hypothesized linear relationship between monitoring and risk reduction has grown steadily in the last decades. Most criticisms cluster around the concepts of "overparenting," "psychological control," "self-determination theory," "social domain theory" and "parental knowledge." Each of these concepts highlights different problems of the monitoring concept. The cumulative effect has led to the claim that the construct has lost its coherence and applicability (Stattin, Kerr & Tilton-Weaver, 2010). A review of those criticisms will show us why we need a new concept and what are the challenges it must face.

Overparenting

The term "overparenting" connotes excessive or developmentally inappropriate parental involvement in a child's life (Segrin, Woszidlo, Givertz & Montgomery, 2013). Historically, the concept of overparenting reflects a transformation of the one-time popular concept of "overprotective mothering." The two concepts differ, but also overlap. This is made clear when we consider the bridging concept of "overprotective parenting," which scholars coined when cultural changes brought about larger involvement of fathers in child rearing. The sequence—overprotective mothering, overprotective parenting and overparenting—reveals a gradual shift in cultural norms: The first term denoted an abnormal mother–child relationship that scholars assumed stemmed from the mother's pathological needs and warped the child's development (Levi, 1943; Parker & Lipscombe, 1981; Thomasgard & Metz, 1993). The second term pointed to a widening of the phenomenon, as more and more fathers joined the ranks of the overprotective (Hastings et al., 2008; Overbeek, ten Have, Vollebergh & de Graaf, 2007). The third term denotes a more recent and assumedly less pathological parenting style influenced by psychological or pop-psychological recommendations for close and continuous involvement between parent and child as a way of guaranteeing positive development. In spite of those differences, the impact of these various kinds of parental over-engagement is similar. This is probably due to the fact that the parents denoted by these terms hover continuously over the child, remaining involved in virtually all of his doings. This "hovering" has given rise to the latest popular term describing the phenomenon: "helicopter parenting" (Padilla-Walker & Nelson, 2012; Willoughby, Hersh, Padilla-Walker & Nelson, 2013).

Scholars described overprotective parents as having: (a) high levels of anxiety regarding the child; (b) difficulty separating from the child; (c) little capacity to encourage autonomous functioning; and (d) high need to monitor and control the child (Thomasgard & Metz, 1993). Research and clinical observations of the children of overprotective parents tended to show lack of autonomy, reduced sense of competence, greater risk for anxiety disorders, and external rather than internal locus of control (Gere, Villabø, Torgersen & Kendall, 2012; Janssens, Oldehinkel & Rosmalen, 2009; Levi, 1943; Spokas & Heimberg, 2009; Thomasgard & Metz, 1993, 1997; Ungar, 2009; Wood, 2006). Most of the literature on overprotective parenting has a psychopathological tone, regarding both the causes and effects of the phenomenon. Thus, among the putative causes of the phenomenon are parental anxiety disorders, a narcissistic personality, a pathological relationship of the parents to their own parents, or a major threat to the child during pregnancy, infancy or early childhood (De Ocampo, Macias, Saylor & Katikaneni, 2003; Levi, 1943; Mullins et al., 2007; Munich & Munich, 2009; Parker & Lipscombe, 1981; Thomasgard, 1998; Thomasgard & Metz, 1997).

In contrast, scholars tend to describe overparenting, or helicopter parenting, as positively rather than pathologically motivated (Padilla-Walker & Nelson, 2012; Segrin, Woszidlo, Givertz, Bauer & Taylor-Murphy, 2012; Shoup, Gonyea & Kuh, 2009; Wartman & Savage, 2008). The professional and especially the popular literature have praised, if not idealized, continuous parental involvement. Bernstein and Triger (2011) described three main characteristics of these parents: (a) They gather information from books and specialists about child growth and children's needs so as to be sensitive to each and every developmental change; (b) they continuously assess the child's strengths and weaknesses, organize his or her free time, and intervene in the child's favor in scholastic and social frames; and (c) they continuously monitor the child's doings and whereabouts. Overparenting is also a product of our age, in that electronics play a central role in allowing for more possibilities of parental involvement. The smartphone, for instance, besides allowing for continuous contact, also enables monitoring of the child's social life and whereabouts (Bernstein & Triger, 2011; Lemoyne & Buchanan, 2011; Shoup et al., 2009). Overparenting tends to continue beyond adolescence as parents remain highly involved in the child's academic (Bernstein & Triger, 2011; Hunt, 2008; Lemoyne & Buchanan, 2011; Padilla-Walker & Nelson, 2012) or even military life (Israel-Ashvili, 1992, 2006).

In spite of the differences in the description of overparenting and overprotective parenting, we believe that many if not most parents who had once fallen into the overprotective category would now fit within the larger category of overparenting, thus shedding some of their pathological aura. The research on the effects of overparenting reinforces this view. Among the problematic consequences researchers have linked to overparenting are (a) lack of autonomy, reduced self-confidence and reduced problem-solving skills (Fischer, Forthun, Pidcock & Dowd, 2007; Segrin et al., 2012); (b) increased anxiety, decreased well-being and excessive use of painkillers (Bayer, Sanson & Hemphill, 2006; Bernstein & Triger, 2011; Lemoyne & Buchanan, 2011; Montgomery, 2010); and (c) increased parent–child conflict and reduced satisfaction with family relations (Segrin et al., 2012). Though possibly lesser in measure, those negative consequences are similar to those that were attributed to overprotective parenting. We interpret this as suggesting that all of those parents engage, among other things, in excessive or inappropriate monitoring, so the child does not have enough space to develop a sense of autonomy and self-confidence.

Taken together, the literature on overprotective parenting and overparenting offers a critical perspective on the assumed linear connection between monitoring and risk. Although monitoring probably helps prevent substance abuse, unsafe sex, problematic peer associations, delinquency, truancy and the like, excessive monitoring (as manifested in overparenting or overprotective parenting) may be linked to an increase in developmental risks, such as an impaired sense of competence and autonomy, less developed problem-solving skills and higher anxiety. We conclude that the concept of monitoring fails to address the need to avoid both under- and overparenting. This is one of the challenges that the concept of vigilant care should address.

Psychological and Behavioral Control

In the 1990s, scholars differentiated two kinds of parental control, psychological and behavioral (for an historic perspective on those concepts, see Soenens & Vansteenkiste, 2010), which were supposed to manifest different motivations and practices. "Psychological control" reflects parental intrusiveness and attempts to manipulate the child through induction of negative feelings, whereas "behavioral control" reflects clear definition and maintenance of rules and limits (Barber & Harmon, 2002). Traditionally, scholars equated behavioral control with parental monitoring and viewed this as an important and protective parenting practice, while assuming that psychological control plays mainly a negative role in child development (Barber, 1996; Barber & Harmon, 2002; Pettit et al., 2001; Steinberg, 2005).

Psychological and behavioral control reputedly represented different dimensions in parenting style. Thus, at the opposite pole of high psychological control, we find parents who allow their child a sense of autonomy and competence, whereas at the opposite pole of high behavioral control, we find parents who fail to give their child a minimum of rules and limits. High psychological control was linked to the development of internalizing disorders, and low behavioral control (or lack of monitoring) to externalizing ones (Barber, Olsen & Shagle, 1994; Wang, Pomerantz & Chen, 2007).

Research only partially supports this distinction. Studies showed that the child may experience high levels of monitoring, or behavioral control, as indistinguishable from psychological control (Kakihara, Tilton-Weaver, Kerr & Stattin, 2010; Rote & Smetana, 2015; Smetana, Villalobos, Tasopoulos-Chan, Gettman & Campione-Barr, 2009), leading to similar relational and developmental sequelae (Stone et al., 2013). In addition, psychological control (at least in moderation) may cause positive effects like those of behavioral control. Thus, psychological control may help the child achieve positive goals, such as preventing negative peer associations (Soenens, Vansteenkiste & Niemiec, 2009), and behavioral control may negatively affect how children feel and think (Wang et al., 2007). Those findings undermine the neat and positive identification of parental monitoring with behavioral control. Control, either behavioral or psychological, may be more or less harmful. Two models attempt to explain when and why control may go astray.

Social Domain and Self-Determination Theory

Studies inspired by social domain theory have shown that the child's negative experience of parental control is not only a function of parenting style in itself, but also of the child's feeling that the domain in which the parents manifest involvement is of a personal and intimate nature (Nucci, 2001; Rote & Smetana, 2015; Smetana & Daddis, 2002). As the child grows, the domains so experienced become wider, leading to the feeling that parental involvement in those areas is invasive and controlling (Smetana & Daddis, 2002). Many adolescents take an uncompromising stance regarding parental involvement in what they view as personal areas, even when these involve risk activities. For instance, adolescents who are involved with bad company may view their choice of friends and social activities as out of bounds for parents, or turn their own room and computer into taboo territories to be defended by all possible means. On the other hand, when adolescents come to feel that the parents' intervention is justified by clear and specific concerns for their safety, they tend to view that intervention as legitimate (Padilla-Walker, Nelson & Knapp, 2014). The parents, too, feel the need for a convincing legitimization, without which they may lack the courage to intervene (Guttman & Gesser-Edelsburg, 2011). The injunction that parents should exercise monitoring in a decided way, without taking care to legitimize their involvement, may thus prove problematic, as it does little to address either the child's resistance or the parents' doubts.

Self-determination theory has provided further qualification to the neat distinction between psychological and behavioral control and the identification of parental monitoring with the latter (Deci & Ryan, 1985; Ryan & Deci, 2000; Soenens & Vansteenkiste, 2010). Parents can provide rules and limits non-invasively and supportively or in a controlling and coercive manner. The proponents of self-determination theory referred to the first possibility as the provision of structure (Grolnick & Pomerantz, 2009). When parents provide rules and limits as structure rather than as controlling impositions, children's ability to accept them grows. The question is then not only *what* the parents do, but also *how* they do it. Thus, when parents exercise monitoring in a controlling spirit, that monitoring impinges on the child's need for self-determination, negatively affecting the child's development and the parent–child relationship. On the other hand, if parents exercise monitoring as structure and in ways that are, as much as possible, free from controlling messages, its effects will be positive.

Evidence from parental training in non-violent resistance (Omer, 2004), in which parents learn to manifest presence and to resist aggressive and self-destructive behaviors in non-violent and non-escalating ways, supports the position that parents can define structure without intimations of control, leading to greater acceptance and less conflict (Lavi-Levavi, Shachar & Omer, 2013; Weinblatt & Omer, 2008). For example, when parents present rules and limits, while taking care to tell the child that it is their duty to do so, but that they cannot dictate the child's feelings, thoughts or acts, they open a path to cooperation. In one study, when the researcher asked children why they cooperated, they often answered: "Because I wanted!" or, "Because it was right for me!" This was interpreted as indicating that the children cooperated out of a feeling of autonomy. Questions regarding positive monitoring should thus concern not only the right degree but also the legitimization of parental involvement. Specifically, (a) how can parents legitimize their increased involvement in problem-fraught areas that the child views as pertaining to his personal domain? and (b) how can parents construct the interaction in such a way that the child's experience is one of structure rather than of control? The concept of vigilant care should be able to address those issues.

Parental Knowledge

In their seminal work, Stattin and Kerr (Kerr & Stattin, 2000; Stattin & Kerr, 2000) scrutinized the concept of parental monitoring, casting doubt on the assumed connection between tracking and surveillance and risk reduction. They argued that the usual questionnaires did not measure parental monitoring, but parental knowledge. Next, they broke down the sources of parental knowledge, as figured in the very questionnaires that purportedly measured parental monitoring, into three components: (a) child disclosure (stemming mainly from an atmosphere of openness and trust), (b) parental solicitation (as shown in focused questioning and tracking) and (c) parental control (as manifested by rules and sanctions). The components of solicitation and control refer to behaviors parents initiate, thus adhering to the original monitoring construct. Disclosure, however, refers to an activity that the child initiates and would thus not fall under the classic view of monitoring (Stattin & Kerr, 2010).

To make matters worse for the monitoring model, spontaneous disclosure turned out to be the chief contributor to parental knowledge and risk prevention, while parental solicitation or control played a minor and sometimes detrimental role (Kerr & Stattin, 2000; Stattin & Kerr, 2000). Those findings greatly affect our understanding of parental monitoring and risk prevention (Racz & McMahon, 2011). The focus on parental knowledge indicates that a dyadic view in which child and parents influence each other mutually should replace the unilateral model of parental monitoring (Laird et al., 2003; Pardini, 2008). Once again, the linear model of parental monitoring is held to be unduly simplistic. The model of vigilant care should be sensitive to the interactive aspects that regulate parental activity. Parents should be helped to develop an atmosphere that furthers spontaneous disclosure, while remaining able to move to more active involvement in case of need.

Cumulative Effects of the Critique

Summing up: The thesis of an inverse linear relationship between monitoring and risk gained support over the years, covering a large range of risk behaviors. The evidence and the resulting injunction ("Monitor your child!") seemed to create a rare occasion in which academic research had simple and clear implications for parenting. For a time, every sign in the field of parental guidance seemed to be pointing in the same direction. Gradually, however, several critical perspectives on the relationship between monitoring and positive development gained traction. First, studies on overparenting challenged the linearity of the relationship, showing that too much monitoring can harm rather than help. Second, the literature on control, and, more specifically, studies inspired by personal domain and self-determination theory, raised the issues of legitimization and control as opposed to structure. Third, research on parental knowledge highlighted the one-sidedness of the monitoring hypothesis and the need to consider the child's spontaneous contribution to parental knowledge.

While such criticisms posed serious challenges for the monitoring paradigm, it was the methodological aspect of Stattin and Kerr's work that turned them into a full-blown crisis. Those authors elegantly demonstrated that the conclusions of the research on monitoring were, in fact, built upon an artifact: In measuring monitoring, one might be, in fact, measuring knowledge, knowledge that might not be the result of monitoring at all. We believe, however, that some of the implications of this shift for the field of parental guidance have not been fully appreciated.

Stattin and Kerr divided the once-straightforward concept of parental monitoring into three components: child disclosure, parental solicitation and parental control. The question then arose of what the relationship was between these factors, and to what extent each of them should receive credit for the robust effects of the monitoring literature. This question was a call for dismantling research, i.e., for studies examining each component separately to isolate the respective effects. Gradually, researchers established a dichotomy between parental knowledge acquired through spontaneous disclosure on the one hand and unilateral monitoring behaviors (solicitation and control) on the other. Some studies tended to adopt an either/or stance regarding the desired kind of parental involvement (Kerr & Stattin, 2003; Kerr, Stattin & Burk, 2010), or at least reflected the suspicion that spontaneous disclosure and unilateral monitoring did not go together (Fletcher, Steinberg & Williams-Wheeler, 2004).

Thus, some studies supported the spontaneous-disclosure component of parental knowledge to the detriment of the solicitation and control components, thus echoing the zeitgeist, which emphasizes the importance of child autonomy (Keijsers, Frijns, Branje & Meeus, 2009; Kerr et al., 2010). Researchers have listed a number of variables that favor spontaneous disclosure, such as positive interactions between parents and child (Willoughby & Hamza, 2011); positive reactions to the child's previous disclosures (Hayes, Hudson & Matthews, 2007; Tilton-Weaver et al., 2010); and the creation of an atmosphere of trust (Smetana, Metzger, Gettman & Campione-Barr, 2006; Smetana & Metzger, 2008).

However, other studies did not support the exclusive endorsement of spontaneous disclosure, as opposed to solicitation and control. Thus, findings show that adolescents spontaneously disclosed information only on a minority of issues, upon which they and their parents agreed (Darling, Cumsille & Dowdy, 2006). Adolescents conceal information for many reasons: to protect a friend, to avoid revealing experimentation with drugs or alcohol, to avoid revealing transgressions against parental norms or even simply to feel independent (Marshall, Tilton-Weaver & Bosdet, 2005; Smetana et al., 2006).

Lying and secrecy are clear predictors of anti-social behavior (Frijns, Keijsers, Branje & Meeus, 2010), and parents' ability to maintain a good level of parental knowledge in spite of lying is a predictor of lesser risk (Bourdeau, Miller, Duke & Ames, 2011; Laird et al., 2003; Waizenhofer, Buchanan & Jackson-Newsom, 2004). Thus, at least when there are signs that point to lying, parents should no longer depend solely on spontaneous disclosure. Moreover, parental solicitation and tracking may not only *not* discourage spontaneous disclosure, but also, under certain conditions, encourage it, as the child adapts positively to parents' vigilance (Fletcher et al., 2004; Laird, Marrero, Melching & Kuhn, 2013; Soenens,

Vansteenkiste, Luyckx & Goossens, 2006). Hence, disclosure might not always be fully "spontaneous."

Specifically, studies have supported the role of active monitoring steps with populations at risk. For example, parental solicitation, tracking, and rule setting were found to be helpful, over and beyond the knowledge parents obtained through spontaneous disclosure, with families who lived in difficult neighborhoods (Lahey, Van Hulle, D'Onofrio, Rodgers & Waldman, 2008), where the children spent a large part of their free time on their own (Coley et al., 2004; Laird, Marrero & Sentse, 2010; Stattin & Kerr, 2000), or with children in risk groups (Fosco, Stormshak, Dishion & Winter, 2012; Hayes et al., 2004; Keijsers et al., 2009; Pettit & Laird, 2002).

Training effects support this contention: helping parents to improve their active monitoring skills with children at risk led to reductions in risk behavior (Lochman & van den Steenhoven, 2002; Vitaro, Brendgen & Tremblay, 2001). Researchers also found that if parents react to the child's extreme reactions by withdrawing from their active monitoring attempts, the child's risk level increases (Kerr, Stattin & Pakalniskiene, 2008; Stattin et al., 2010). Assisting parents in maintaining unilateral vigilant behavior in the face of adversity, especially in cases where clear signs of alarm are forthcoming, might well be a major challenge for parental intervention programs.

The literature thus supports different parental attitudes in a variety of situations and with different populations. The question is whether this heterogeneous picture can be integrated into a coherent model. Without such an integration, research may remain confusing, with more and more papers pointing in different directions in ways that are less and less helpful for parents and practitioners alike. This fragmentation poses a problem not only from a practical, but also a scientific point of view, as science should aim at parsimony (i.e., Occam's razor). Ideally, after dismantling research has succeeded in undermining an oversimplification, researchers must find a way toward integration.

Crisis of Fragmentation

For many years, the central assumptions of the monitoring model dominated research and practice with virtually no competitors. The model has withstood its share of criticisms, managing to carry their burden for a duration. However, the work of Stattin and Kerr (2000), revealing a pervasive artifact in the very evidence that sustained the model, has created a new situation, in which the cumulative criticisms can no longer be contained within the extant framework. In fact, a major flaw that is disclosed in the methodological basis of an approach may be the single worst fate for a scientific theory. In his classical description on how theories withstand criticisms or crumble under their weight, Kuhn (1970) has specifically mentioned how the disclosure of flaws in measurement methodology may galvanize "anomalies," turning them into a fullblown "crisis" (pp. 5, 83).

The crisis, if we may so term it, has reopened the relatively wide consensus regarding the monitoring–risk relationship, almost inverting some aspects of the assumed connection. The positive results that researchers first viewed as stemming from unilateral parental monitoring are now viewed as indicating knowledge that is mainly due to spontaneous disclosure by the child (Stattin et al., 2010). Gradually, the very use of the term monitoring has come to require additions or clarifications. One interesting example is the hybrid "monitoring knowledge" (Hayes et al., 2004). This term has been justly criticized as increasing the confusion (Racz & McMahon, 2011; Stattin et al., 2010). What seems clear, however, is that the concept of monitoring can no longer do the job (Stattin et al., 2010).

The theoretical crisis has profound practical effects. Earlier, when the monitoring model reigned, research seemed easily translatable into practical guidelines. Parents needed to develop and maintain high levels of monitoring. With the model's weakening and the growing heterogeneity of research, practical injunctions have become fragmented, not to say contradictory (Kerr et al., 2010). Trust is vital, but so is unilateral checking and tracking. Parental involvement is crucial, but so are personal domains and self-determination. Solicitation abets disclosure, but also hinders it. How do parents know what to do? This precarious situation calls for integration.

Calls for Integration

On the basis of the extant evidence, a number of researchers have argued that knowledge based on disclosure does not replace the active steps traditionally subsumed under parental monitoring, but that both factors exist side-by-side and may have synergistic effects (Fletcher et al., 2004; Hamza & Willoughby, 2011; Hayes et al., 2004; Keijsers & Laird, 2014; Lippold, Greenberg & Collins, 2013, 2014; Soenens et al., 2006). Those authors have intimated that viewing spontaneous disclosure and active monitoring steps as distinct or as mutually competitive was a mistake. Fostering open dialogue, while having recourse to tracking and structuring, can and should constitute a continuous parenting process. An integrative model should offer us applicable and empirically supported ways of combining unilateral moves with openness and dialogue in the best possible way.

Over the past few years, we have witnessed some initial attempts at integration. For instance, using the person-oriented approach, Lippold et al. (2013, 2014) examined combinations of different behaviors as they appear in parent–child dyads. Instead of focusing on various parental behaviors separately, these authors looked at how parents combine different behaviors, how these combinations relate to outcome, and how the combinations change as the child grows. For instance, they replicated the known finding that parents' unilateral monitoring behaviors decline over time, but they also showed that when the parents of younger children are high both in open communication and supervision, the decline of unilateral monitoring in later years is much less pronounced and risk remains lower (Lippold et al., 2014). Although the authors did not offer a general integrative model, they presented their research as an attempt to cope with the field's state of fragmentation.

The present work highlights the need to characterize the continuum of attention and action whereby parents foster an atmosphere of openness, detect warning signs, focus their attention when such signs appear and intervene actively when the child participates in damaging activities. Spelling out how and when an open and positive interest in the child could pave the way for effective solicitation and structure, and vice-versa, are some of the challenges for the required integrative model. We believe that the field is ripe for the introduction of such a model. Accordingly, the goal of the vigilant care model is to offer an answer to the dilemmas raised by criticisms of parental monitoring, to incorporate the richness and variety of the findings on parental involvement and risk reduction and to offer a comprehensive and scientifically informed program of action that parents can understand, accept and implement.

Vigilant Care

The term monitoring, with its mechanical associations, implies an attitude that contrasts with the kind of atmosphere that many parents and professionals would like to foster. In a way, the term is anachronistic. It connotes inspection and control, thus raising associations with an authoritarian rather than an authoritative parenting style. The critical evidence we have reviewed supports this view, showing that parents often solicit information and impose rules in ways that may lead to increased hostility and distancing. To our minds, this and the other criticism we reviewed cannot be accommodated by a redefinition or re-operationalization of the term parental monitoring, or by its replacement with parental knowledge. We require a new concept.

Vigilant care is a flexible attitude in which parents shift between levels of open attention, focused attention and protective action, according to the alarm signals they detect. At the level of open attention, parents manifest a non-intrusive, caring interest in the child, while also establishing non-inquisitive contacts and communication with people in the child's environment (e.g., teachers, friends or other parents). So long as there are no particular warning signs, the parents stay at this level. By setting open attention as the "default" level of parental involvement, parents create conditions that may best favor spontaneous disclosure and open dialogue (Tilton-Weaver, 2014; Tilton-Weaver et al., 2010). If, however, such signs become evident (e.g., the child lies, scholastic achievements recede or problematic friendships develop), the parents increase their involvement by acts of focused attention. At this level, they start tracking and asking the child about the particulars of his activities. They also clarify and reassert rules left in abeyance. If the alarm signs recede, the parents reduce unilateral solicitation and return to open attention. If, however, the child still engages in problematic activities, they advance to active protection, adding active steps to reduce the danger. This graded approach allows the parents to pursue a series of connected aims: (a) by staying mostly at the lowest level of vigilance (i.e., open attention), they foster an atmosphere of trust and autonomy, thus increasing the chances for spontaneous disclosure; (b) by learning to cultivate open attention, they increase the chances that they will notice alarm signs; (c) by their readiness to move to focused attention and protective steps in case of need, they show that they remain present and do not abdicate their parental role, even when the child tries to create distance and concealment; (d) by regulating their level of trust according to the alarm signs they detect, they allow the child to feel that the levels of trust and independence he is allowed is a function of his behavior; (e) by linking the introduction of unilateral steps (i.e., focused attention and protective steps) to obvious signs of danger, they increase the legitimacy of those moves; and (f) by moving to higher levels only when conditions clearly require that they do so, they keep themselves from invasiveness and overparenting.

The parents' activity at each level serves as a platform that facilitates transition to other levels: open attention potentiates focused attention and protective steps, while a respectful exercise of focused attention and protective steps potentiates a safe return to open attention. The three elements that constitute parental knowledge (disclosure, solicitation and structure), rather than being potentially detrimental to each other (Kerr et al., 2010), are made continuous and mutually supportive (Soenens et al., 2006). Under those conditions, the parents do not leave the level of open attention when they move to upper levels, but maintain both levels concomitantly. The model predicts that if parents move to upper levels correctly, they create the conditions for a mutual potentiation between one-sided parental moves and spontaneous disclosure (Lippold et al., 2013, 2014).

Parents of very young children spontaneously evince the continuous adjustments of vigilant care. For instance, a mother with a baby stays mainly at the level of open attention when the baby is calm or asleep, moves to focused attention if the child shows signs of distress and shifts to active protection if the distress persists. Similarly, a father who takes his child to the playground remains openly attentive when the child plays in the sandbox, moves to focused attention if a dog comes near and takes protective action if the child cries or the dog growls. These examples show that the shifts between different levels are, in fact, natural to parents. Similar adjustments are called for with older children, taking into consideration the child's growing need for autonomy and the fact that an older child may resist parental intervention. Through these adjustments, the parents allow the child a safe space for experimentation. By being "left alone under the parents' eyes," the child can safely practice new skills and develop a sense of autonomy. Thus, a baby who is left by herself with the mother close by begins to learn how to soothe herself, and a child who is allowed space to cope with routine challenges develops the ability to do so independently. Parents learn to check themselves for overparenting by asking themselves whether they are not moving to higher levels unjustifiably. The injunction to stay at the lowest level, unless warning signs appear, helps them counter the tendency to overparent. This kind of inner dialogue is encouraged so that parents who tend to overparent may change their attitude into one of graded vigilant care. Indeed, when parents are offered a clear way to exercise vigilant care (e.g., are trained to recognize alarm signals and helped to react with appropriate involvement), they feel more secure that they are not neglecting the child when they reduce their vigilance level.

In the model of vigilant care, the active risk-reducing ingredient is not assumed to be control (either behavioral or psychological), but *parental presence* (Omer, 2004, 2012, 2015; Omer et al., 2013). In the traditional monitoring model, scholars viewed prevention of risk as a function of the parents' ability to achieve control over the child's behavior. The assumption in vigilant care differs completely: Parents cannot control the child's behavior (even less so the child's feelings or thoughts). In other eras or societies, parents were perhaps more able to dictate the child's actions because their ability to compel was almost unlimited. Even then, however, parents were only able to enforce the desired behavior so long as the child was under their direct observation. Once the child was away, they had no control. Many children will exhibit compliance when observed or threatened, only to make sure they do the exact opposite when away from parents' eyes.

What parents can do, however, is to give the child a sense of accompaniment, by staying close or being present in the child's mind. Presence is more direct and immediate when the child is small, becoming more indirect and virtual as the child grows. By being present to the child, first physically and, in later years, more and more mentally, parents help the child internalize their care; vigilant care can thus be gradually transformed into self-care. Control, in contrast, if it were at all possible, would not be internalized so easily (Grolnick, 2002). Adolescents who are forced to do something do not usually internalize the controlling agency. On the contrary, they often do all they can to evade it, so as best to assert their self-determination (Kochanska & Aksan, 2006; Soenens & Vansteenkiste, 2010).

Understanding that the active mechanism in vigilant care is not control but presence has highly practical implications. Parents who understand that they cannot control the child, but, at best, only themselves, learn to reduce messages that imply control. Studies have shown that this shift in parental attitude paves the way for cooperation (Lavi-Levavi et al., 2013; Shimshoni et al., 2015). In effect, control is not just a putative mechanism of monitoring (Gray & Steinberg, 1999), but a problematic parental goal and form of communication (Soenens & Vansteenkiste, 2010). Helping parents relinquish the goal of control and its concomitant controlling messages in favor of messages of parental presence and commitment to the child's safety reduces escalation and increases the chances for cooperation. Indeed, adolescents have been shown to be more willing to accept parental limits and demands when clearly linked to prudential areas (Padilla-Walker et al., 2014). The understanding that prevention of risk is often mediated by the parent's presence in the child's mind clarifies the probable effectiveness of some parental steps that would be meaningless under the assumption that control was the mediating factor. Thus, when the mother of an adolescent drops her off at the house where she will be staying overnight, the very fact that the mother knows where the house is located, and that she took the girl to the door of the house, creates a degree of presence in the child's mind that would be absent if the girl had arrived on her own or had been driven by others. This mental parental presence may then help inhibit participation in forbidden activities. Various programs of vigilant care have used the establishment of a virtual parental presence in the child's mind, for instance, to diminish aggressive driving (Shimshoni et al., 2015) or decrease risk behaviors of delinquent adolescents under peer pressure (Omer, 2015). On this view, it is probably not the parents' actual knowledge, but rather their presence in the child's mind, that contributes best to the child's ability to withstand temptation.

Programs of vigilant care have been variously adapted to deal with lying, bad company, violence, truancy, cigarettes, alcohol, drugs, unsafe sex, computer misuse, school refusal, juvenile diabetes, theft and dangerous driving (Omer, 2015). In all of those fields, the programs defined parental steps for each of the three levels of vigilant care and specified rules for how and when the parents should shift between levels. Those programs drew from previous experience on how to help parents cope with violent and self-destructive behaviors through non-violent resistance, which involves a combination of decided parental presence, prevention of escalation, and minimization of control messages (Lavi-Levavi et al., 2013; Newman, Fagan & Webb, 2014; Ollefs, Schlippe, Omer & Kriz, 2009; Omer, 2004; Weinblatt & Omer, 2008).

Open Attention

Clara began to worry when Mira (13) started partying and began to come home late. Mira was a responsible child with an open relationship with her mother. Clara hesitated, because on the one side, she didn't want to be overcontrolling, but on the other side, she felt the parties were a new phase in Mira's development in which she might be exposed to new kinds of temptations. Clara talked to a friend, whose daughter was in the same class as Mira. Her friend suggested that Clara take Mira to a "girls' talk" in a coffee shop. "Girls' talk" was a familiar term in a family where besides Clara and Mira there were only males around (besides the father, there were three brothers). After a few minutes in the coffee shop, Clara said: "I want to talk with you about the parties, but I am not going to sermonize you. I trust you. But I would like to tell you how I felt when I started to go to parties, so that if you experience similar situations, you may trust me too." For the first time in her life, Clara told Mira about her own experiences as a teenager. Mira was very interested, and told Clara about two of the girls in her class who already had boyfriends. Clara asked Mira to come to her if she had any doubts or troubles. Mira nodded uncommittedly. Clara felt that although Mira had not made her any promises, an opening had been created that might make it easier for Mira to ask Clara for help in case of need.

Focused Attention

One year after his divorce, Maurice started noticing changes in the behavior of his son, Gabriel (17). When he slept over at his father's, Gabriel would often absent himself for hours or come back very late without notifying his father. Maurice felt this was the result of a weakening in his parental function, a process that had begun a few years back and had been aggravated by the stress of the divorce and his fear of losing his son's affection. Maurice decided that he had to change his attitude if he wanted to keep Gabriel from getting into trouble. When Gabriel next returned at two o'clock in the morning, he found his father waiting for him in the hall. He said: "Tomorrow we'll have a talk about the rules regarding your outings." Gabriel began to raise his voice in protest, but Maurice told him: "I don't want to talk now, because both you and I are not in the condition to have a good conversation. We'll talk tomorrow when I come back from work." In the morning, Maurice called Gabriel from his workplace to remind him of their date. On coming home, Maurice asked Gabriel to sit with him in his office. He told Gabriel that in the last year there had been a slackening of the rules, but now a change was needed because of Gabriel's disappearances and late comings. From now on, he would ask Gabriel to inform him every time where he was going, with whom and when he was coming back. In case Gabriel for some reason could not return at the agreed time, he should call and explain the reason for his delay. Gabriel protested, claiming that his father was depriving him of his privacy. Maurice answered: "So long as you give me this minimal information and keep the hours we stipulate, I won't bother you. But as things have developed, I have to ask you those questions!" In the following weeks, Maurice started to ask Gabriel every day about his plans for the evening. He would also call him from work, to enquire when he was leaving. Maurice avoided interrogating Gabriel at length, keeping the conversations short and to the point. When Gabriel protested again and went into a prolonged sulk, Gabriel's uncle James, who had a positive relationship with him, called him, told him he knew about the new rules and added: "Gabriel, that's a very reasonable demand! What do you want? That your dad give up on you? He'll never do that; neither will I!" After a halting start, Gabriel adapted himself to the new rules. Maurice felt that the chaotic family situation had begun to stabilize.

Protective Action

Shirley found out that Eva (11) had lied to her when she told her there was an after-hours school activity that day. She also found that Eva had stolen money from her purse. She decided to check what exactly was going on and called three of Eva's close friends. When the third one answered elusively, Shirley decided to call her mother. The mother told her that she had taken both girls to the movies. Eva had lied because Shirley had not allowed her to go to that movie, which she thought inappropriate for a girl her age. Shirley did not hesitate: she came to the cinema, explained to the usher that her daughter was inside without her permission, entered the projection room, found Eva, took her out and brought her home with her. Shirley kept silent during the drive home. When they arrived, she told Eva that they would have a serious talk in the evening, after the father's return from work.

Privacy, Trust and Spying

The understanding that vigilant care is a flexible attitude, that can become looser or tighter in accordance with the situation, helps solve two related dilemmas: (a) How can vigilant care be reconciled with the child's need for privacy? (b) How can vigilant care be reconciled with the child's need for trust? The answer to these questions is basically the same. With time, the child's sphere of privacy grows and vigilant care stays more and more at the level of open attention, but only if there are no obvious alarm signs and the child seems to be watching over herself. Similarly, the child will gain more trust, and the need for focused attention and protective action will diminish, if she abstains from dissimulation and supplies reliable information. These rules help parents regulate their vigilant care in both directions, enabling them to tighten or loosen it, according to need.

One of the paradoxes of modern society is that precisely at a time when young people are exposed to more and more temptations, and endless possibilities for clandestine and anonymous activities are offered by the vast urban spaces and the internet, the value of privacy has become sacrosanct, so that the slightest threat of its curtailment is regarded as absolutely unacceptable. Parents often behave as if they were ruled by a "privacy reflex." This is the tendency to refrain from any parental activity the moment the slightest innuendo is raised that it may impinge on the child's privacy. The very mention of a possible infringement of privacy in sayings like, "This is my room!" "This is my money!" "Those are my friends!" paralyzes the parents, even when the child's activities in her room, with her money or her friends are highly suspicious. Privacy is, of course, a central value in our society. The privacy reflex, however, turns privacy into an untouchable right that cannot be weighed in relation to vital values, like the duty to guarantee the child's safety.

The Privacy Reflex

Sid found out that his daughter Venus (12) had been visiting pornographic sites on her laptop, which she had received as a "consolation present" from her grandmother on account of her parents' divorce. Venus would brag that she visited porno sites, as if this was her unalienable right, because the computer belonged to her. Perhaps her bragging was actually a call for help. Sid did not dare to intervene, fearing this might threaten the delicate balance that had been achieved in his relationship with his daughter and his ex-wife. He felt that the laptop, being a present from the maternal grandmother, was doubly out of bounds for him, both as Venus' personal property and as a present from the maternal side. His sense of paralysis and worry for his daughter brought him to counseling. The counselor backed him in taking steps against the girl's exposure, and helped him build up a group of supporters (relatives and friends), who legitimized his steps. With this help, Sid became able to take action: he confiscated the laptop, expunged the porno downloads and, for a time, allowed his daughter to surf the Web only under his supervision. With the help of one of the supporters, he sent a message to his ex-wife, who upheld his decision. To his surprise, after a mild protest, Venus accepted the new rule and gave up her dangerous hobby.

Most parents rightly feel that trust is a valuable element in their relationship with their child. In effect, when the child earns the parent's trust by his behavior, candidness and ability to watch over himself, trust is a highly constructive element in his development. However, it is not true that every child must feel that his parents trust him unconditionally in order to develop well. On the contrary, a child who gets into risk and hides his acts is in need of a parent who is able to give him *less* trust, in order to develop well. This understanding is hard for many parents, who, even after repeated violations of their trust, try again and again "to open a new page" with the child. These attempts usually achieve no more than exposing the child to strong temptations and increasing the parents' disappointment when they find their trust abused. A more appropriate parental attitude in these cases is one of limited trust, in which trust is regulated according to the situation. Thus, when the child is willing to supply information and abides by his agreements with the parent, the parent trusts more and checks less. But if the child refuses to give information or shows signs of dissimulation, the parent trusts less and checks more.

The Trap of Unconditional Trust

Julia (14) was caught a number of times stealing from her mother, Virginia. Julia was isolated in her class and tried to get friends by buying them things. Virginia understood that she should watch closely over her money, as this would help keep Julia from the temptation to steal. She also got in touch with the school counselor, who undertook a number of steps to help Julia out of her isolation. Julia's condition gradually improved. Half a year after the last stealing episode, Virginia told Julia proudly that she now trusted her again and that they would now "open a new page." The announcement was followed by a slackening of her watchfulness. Julia was very glad about the mother's announcement and her behavior continued to improve. However, three months later, when Julia got once again into trouble socially, she resorted yet again to the old remedy of buying friends with stolen money. The mother was totally shocked when she found out. She had a bad outburst, Julia withdrew into her shell and the mother-daughter relationship reached an all-time low.

The principle stipulating that the level of vigilant care should be proportional to the warning signals enables us also to judge where the parent's vigilance is inappropriately intrusive and the child does not get enough space. The typical modalities of inappropriate intrusiveness are *anxious vigilance* and *spying*. Anxious vigilance is shown when, in the absence of warning signs, the parent prevents the child from engaging in important age-appropriate activities, or allows them only under close supervision. Anxious vigilance is not hard to identify. Actually, most such parents openly admit that they are overanxious and unable to withstand situations where they do not know exactly what is happening to their child. Anxiously vigilant parents try to keep their anxiety at bay either by setting up excessive limits on the child's freedom of movement or by questioning the child obsessively and harassingly. Spying parents opt for a different solution: they achieve an illusion of control by getting information behind the child's back. Spying originates from fear and perpetuates fear. A spying parent gets caught in contradictory fears: She spies because she fears bad things might escape her, while also fearing the child might catch her spying. Far from enhancing the parent's capacity to act, spying badly hurts it. Most parents do not dare to act on the evidence they have found, while those who do are beset by an aura of illegitimacy that badly limits their effectiveness. They then act hesitantly or aggressively, or get caught in a web of lies in trying to hide their spying.

The Spying Trap

George was a widower who felt more and more worried that Alice (17) was smoking marijuana with her boyfriend. They used to shut themselves up in her room for hours on end. George noticed that his daughter would sometimes eat ravenously upon coming out of her room. He checked Alice's handbag and found a plastic bag with marijuana. His fear of an open confrontation led him to contrive a convoluted plan. He asked a friend who was a policeman to help him. The friend called Alice and asked her for a meeting because he had something very important to tell her. He told her that she and her boyfriend had been observed by the police. He told her he went to great pains to prevent their arrest, out of friendship for the family. He said that they would continue under observation and that if it transpired they were still using drugs this would lead to their arrest. Alice asked him whether her father knew, and he denied it. He told her that if she abstained completely, her father would not be told. In this roundabout way, George believed he had achieved his goal. However, his standing as a parent was badly hurt by his deception: to avoid an open talk with his daughter, George had engendered a situation in which his daughter believed she was conspiring with the policeman against her father!

The Anchoring Function

One of our cherished beliefs about parenting is that in order for the child to develop well, she should experience a secure and firm attachment. An unconditional loving relationship is the soil from which the growing child draws her resilience and capacity to live a good and fruitful life. This primary bond enables the child to internalize the parents' values and to develop the ability for positive intimate relations. Attachment theory posits that the parent should fulfill the functions of *safe haven* and *secure base* for the growing child (Ainsworth, 1991; Bowlby, 1988). The *safe haven* is symbolized by the parent's open arms and loving hug, that convey acceptance, consolation and encouragement—for instance, when the parent soothingly hugs his child who got scared by a dog, was hurt by a classmate or failed in a competition. The *secure base* complements the function of *safe haven*. The parent serves the child as a *secure base*, when he enables and encourages the child's explorations of her surroundings, in ways that allow the child to develop her skills, knowledge and self-reliance. Examples of the parent's function as a *secure base*: A mother who gently shoves her lingering child into the playground, saying, "I am sitting here and can see you all the time!"; a father who takes his son to a swimming course and waves to him from time to time; a mother who encourages her daughter to undertake her first independent bus ride, telling her she will be available on the phone. The emphasis of the term *secure base* lies in its outward direction; that of *safe haven*, in its inner direction. The parent serves as a *safe haven* when the child *comes back* to the embrace when hurt, tired, lonely or afraid; he serves as a *secure base* when the child *goes out* to new explorations. These functions are the two sides of the same coin. The warm embrace and the mild push are closely linked moves, which further the child's sense of security and independence. However, a third basic element—the *anchoring function*—may be lacking in this description. The *anchoring function* reflects the parent's strength and firmness, by which he can prevent damaging acts on the part of the child (Omer, Guttman-Steinmetz, Carty and von Schlippe, 2013). In the roles of *safe haven* and *secure base*, the parent manifests his sensitive, accepting, understanding and encouraging side. In the *anchoring function*, the parent provides limits and stability. In the first two functions the parent's sensitivity and emotional responsiveness come into play; in the third, his authority. To our mind, the parent–child relationship cannot be stable and safe unless the parent is able to protect himself, the child and their relationship from the storms that puncture the child's growth. Therefore, secure attachment requires both sensitivity and authority. A haven and base will not be safe or secure unless the ship is well anchored, so that it does not hurl itself against the harbor walls or drift unchecked into dangerous waters.

Vigilant care is a major way by which the parents fulfill their *anchoring function*. Because of its flexible nature, vigilant care is like an anchor with a long rope: most of the time the child is free to move, especially as the rope grows longer and longer with the child's growing age. However, it should be clear to the child that the anchor is firmly attached to the ground, ensuring that, in case of need, she will be stopped before she gets hurt. A good anchor does not prevent the development of autonomy or hinder the child from eventually leaving the harbor. When the child is ripe, the anchor is lifted, affixed to the hulk, and the ship sails forth. Similarly, the parent's vigilant care is gradually turned into self-care, a skill that the growing child carries wherever she goes.

Summing up: For years the parental monitoring model enjoyed a special status in the area of risk prevention. However, the concept has gradually lost its appeal, coherence and empirical backing. Research, and its applicability to parenting, suffered more and more from fragmentation. The field seemed ripe for a new model that would address the different lines of criticism and offer a basis for coherent and evidence-based practice. Vigilant care is a flexible framework in which parents adjust their level of involvement to the warning signals they detect. The different levels—open attention, focused attention and protective action—cover a range of parental acts that may bridge the gap between a sensitive–attentive attitude and an authoritative stance regarding risk behaviors. The model views those two attitudes as poles on a continuum of parental involvement. The basic or default level of vigilant care is open attention. This parental stance fosters spontaneous disclosure and the development of autonomy. The move to higher levels of parental involvement occurs when warning signals are detected. The model attributes high importance to the legitimization of parental moves to higher levels, so as to minimize conflict and escalation. The idea is that when parents learn to legitimize those moves in a positive way, the child will experience their involvement as less arbitrary and invasive, and their rules and limits as conveying structure rather than control. Even at the highest level of involvement (active protection), the active ingredient of vigilant care is assumed to be parental presence and not parental control. This accompanying presence is assumed to facilitate internalization, so that parental vigilant care is transformed into self-care. On a larger developmental plane, vigilant care is viewed as furthering the anchoring function that is needed for the development of secure attachment.

The model shows heuristic value through (a) its ability to generate new hypotheses—for instance, that vigilant care promotes internalization, reduces conflict and escalation, leads to higher legitimacy, and reduces control and invasiveness in the eyes of parent and child alike; and (b) its ability to be readily translated into specific programs for different risk conditions. Those characteristics, and the fact that the model takes into account the criticisms that led to the fragmentation of theory, research and practice, make it a promising candidate for alleviating the crisis affecting the field of risk reduction.

The Purpose of This Book

The present book aims to be a guide for professionals who work with parents, on the various levels and domains of vigilant care. Since vigilant care is intuitive, and therefore easier, with smaller children, we shall focus mostly on children of school age and upwards, with a special emphasis on the years of adolescence, in which the parents' difficulties and dilemmas, as well as the dangers for the child, grow apace. We shall ask how parents can foster an open dialogue with a child, so as to get a good feel for what is going on without resorting to the more demanding steps of focused questioning and unilateral actions. We shall ask when the transition to a higher level of vigilant care is not only justified, but necessary. We shall discuss the difficult points in these transitions, so that parents may prepare themselves, build up courage and gain a clear legitimization for their steps. We shall give special attention to the parents' understandable fears that tightening their vigilant care might lead to escalation, arouse sharp reactions and damage their relationship with the child. We shall give close consideration to the problem of adolescents who refuse all cooperation and don't refrain from dissimulation or threats to deter their parents. We shall also focus on specific areas of vigilant care, such as lying, bad company, computer abuse and life-endangering habits. A new field in which we have recently amassed evidence on the effectiveness of vigilant care is that of young drivers. As we shall see, though many young drivers are, at least legally, young adults, driving, at least in the initial months, is a field of manifest danger that does not lie beyond the scope and securing influence of vigilant care.

Notes

1 The gender of pronouns is alternated throughout the book.

References

Ainsworth, M. D. S. (1991). Attachment and other affectional bonds across the life cycle. In C. M. Parkes, J. Stevenson-Hinde & P. Marris (Eds.), *Attachment across the Life Cycle* (pp. 33–51). New York: Routledge.

Barber, B. K. (1996). Parental psychological control: Revisiting a neglected construct. *Child Development*, *67*(6), 3296–3319.

Barber, B. K. & Harmon, E. L. (2002). Violating the self: Parental psychological control of children and adolescents. B. K. Barber (Ed.), *Inclusive Parenting: How psychological control affects children and adolescents* (pp. 15–22). Washington, DC: American Psychological Association.

Barber, B. K., Olsen, J. E. & Shagle, S. C. (1994). Associations between parental psychological and behavioral control and youth internalized and externalized behaviors. *Child Development*, *65*(4), 1120–1136.

Bayer, J. K., Sanson, A. V. & Hemphill, S. A. (2006). Parent influences on early childhood internalizing difficulties. *Journal of Applied Developmental Psychology*, *27*(6), 542–559.

Beck, K. H., Boyle, J. R. & Boekeloo, B. O. (2004). Parental monitoring and adolescent drinking: Results of a 12-month follow-up. *American Journal of Health Behavior*, *28*(3), 272–279.
Bernstein, G. & Triger, Z. (2011). Over-parenting. *UC Davis Law Review*, *44*, 1221–1279.
Bingham, C. R. & Shope, J. T. (2004). Adolescent developmental antecedents of risky driving among young adults. *Journal of Studies on Alcohol and Drugs*, *65*(1), 84.
Bourdeau, B., Miller, B. A., Duke, M. R. & Ames, G. M. (2011). Parental strategies for knowledge of adolescents' friends: Distinct from monitoring? *Journal of Child and Family Studies*, *20*(6), 814–821.
Bowlby, J. (1988). *A Secure Base: Clinical applications of attachment theory*. London: Routledge.
Chamberlain, P. & Reid, J. B. (1998). Comparison of two community alternatives to incarceration for chronic juvenile offenders. *Journal of Consulting and Clinical Psychology*, *66*(4), 624.
Cohen, D. A., Farley, T. A., Taylor, S. N., Martin, D. H. & Schuster, M. A. (2002). When and where do youths have sex? The potential role of adult supervision. *Pediatrics*, *110*(6), e66–e66.
Coley, R. L., Morris, J. E. & Hernandez, D. (2004). Out-of-school care and problem behavior trajectories among low-income adolescents: Individual, family, and neighborhood characteristics as added risks. *Child Development*, *75*(3), 948–965.
Cookston, J. T. (1999). Parental supervision and family structure: Effects on adolescent problem behaviors. *Journal of Divorce & Remarriage*, *32*(1–2), 107–122.
Crouter, A. C., MacDermid, S. M., McHale, S. M. & Perry-Jenkins, M. (1990). Parental monitoring and perceptions of children's school performance and conduct in dual- and single-earner families. *Developmental Psychology*, *26*(4), 649.
Dalton, M. A., Adachi-Mejia, A. M., Longacre, M. R., Titus-Ernstoff, L. T., Gibson, J. J., Martin, S. K., Sargent, J. D. & Beach, M. L. (2006). Parental rules and monitoring of children's movie viewing associated with children's risk for smoking and drinking. *Pediatrics*, *118*(5), 1932–1942.
Darling, N., Cumsille, P., Caldwell, L. L. & Dowdy, B. (2006). Predictors of adolescents' disclosure to parents and perceived parental knowledge: Between-and-within-person differences. *Journal of Youth and Adolescence*, *35*(4), 659–670.
Deci, E. L. & Ryan, R. M. (1985). *Intrinsic Motivation and Self-Determination in Human Behavior*. New York: Plenum Press.
De Ocampo, A. C., Macias, M. M., Saylor, C. F. & Katikaneni, L. D. (2003). Caretaker perception of child vulnerability predicts behavior problems in NICU graduates. *Child Psychiatry and Human Development*, *34*(2), 83–96.
DiClemente, R. J., Wingood, G. M., Crosby, R., Cobb, B. K., Harrington, K. & Davies, S. L. (2001). Parent-adolescent communication and sexual risk behaviors among African American adolescent females. *Journal of Pediatrics*, *139*(3), 407–412.
Dishion, T. J. & McMahon, R. J. (1998). Parental monitoring and the prevention of child and adolescent problem behavior: A conceptual and empirical formulation. *Clinical Child and Family Psychology Review*, *1*(1), 61–75.
Dishion, T. J., Nelson, S. E. & Bullock, B. M. (2004). Premature adolescent autonomy: Parent disengagement and deviant peer process in the amplification of problem behaviour. *Journal of Adolescence*, *27*(5), 515–530.

Ensminger, M. E., Juon, H. S. & Fothergill, K. E. (2002). Childhood and adolescent antecedents of substance use in adulthood. *Addiction*, *97*(7), 833–844.

Fischer, J. L., Forthun, L. F., Pidcock, B. W. & Dowd, D. A. (2007). Parent relationships, emotion regulation, psychosocial maturity and college student alcohol use problems. *Journal of Youth and Adolescence*, *36*(7), 912–926.

Fletcher, A. C., Steinberg, L. & Williams-Wheeler, M. (2004). Parental influences on adolescent problem behavior: Revisiting Stattin and Kerr. *Child Development*, *75*(3), 781–796.

Fosco, G. M., Stormshak, E. A., Dishion, T. J. & Winter, C. E. (2012). Family relationships and parental monitoring during middle school as predictors of early adolescent problem behavior. *Journal of Clinical Child & Adolescent Psychology*, *41*(2), 202–213.

Frijns, T., Keijsers, L., Branje, S. & Meeus, W. (2010). What parents don't know and how it may affect their children: Qualifying the disclosure–adjustment link. *Journal of Adolescence*, *33*(2), 261–270.

Gere, M. K., Villabø, M. A., Torgersen, S. & Kendall, P. C. (2012). Overprotective parenting and child anxiety: The role of co-occurring child behavior problems. *Journal of Anxiety Disorders*, *26*(6), 642–649.

Gray, M. R. & Steinberg, L. (1999). Unpacking authoritative parenting: Reassessing a multidimensional construct. *Journal of Marriage and the Family*, *61*(3), 574–587.

Grolnick, W. S. (2002). *The Psychology of Parental Control: How well-meant parenting backfires*. New York: Psychology Press.

Grolnick, W. S. & Pomerantz, E. M. (2009). Issues and challenges in studying parental control: Toward a new conceptualization. *Child Development Perspectives*, *3*(3), 165–170.

Guttman, N. & Gesser-Edelsburg, A. (2011). "The Little Squealer" or "The Virtual Guardian Angel"? Young drivers' and their parents' perspective on using a driver monitoring technology and its implications for parent–young driver communication. *Journal of Safety Research*, *42*, 51–59.

Hartos, J. L., Eitel, P., Haynie, D. L. & Simons-Morton, B. G. (2000). Can I take the car? Relations among parenting practices and adolescent problem-driving practices. *Journal of Adolescent Research*, *15*(3), 352–367.

Hartos, J., Eitel, P. & Simons-Morton, B. (2002). Parenting practices and adolescent risky driving: A three-month prospective study. *Health Education & Behavior*, *29*(2), 194–206.

Hastings, P. D., Sullivan, C., McShane, K. E., Coplan, R. J., Utendale, W. T. & Vyncke, J. D. (2008). Parental socialization, vagal regulation, and preschoolers' anxious difficulties: Direct mothers and moderated fathers. *Child Development*, *79*(1), 45–64.

Hayes, L., Hudson, A. & Matthews, J. (2004). Parental monitoring behaviors: A model of rules, supervision, and conflict. *Behavior Therapy*, *35*(3), 587–604.

Hayes, L., Hudson, A. & Matthews, J. (2007). Understanding parental monitoring through analysis of monitoring episodes in context. *International Journal of Behavioral Consultation and Therapy*, *3*(1), 96.

Hunt, J. (2008). Make room for daddy... and mommy: Helicopter parents are here. *Journal of Academic Administration in Higher Education*, *4*(1), 9–11.

Israelashvili, M. (1992). *Sharp Turn: A model for the involvement of the educational counselor in the preparation of students for military service* (in Hebrew). Tel Aviv: Ramot.

Israelashvili, M. (2006). The school-to-army transition: Interventions for high-school students and their families. In P. Buchwald (Ed.), *Stress and Anxiety: Application to health, community, work place, and education* (pp. 325–346). Cambridge: Cambridge Scholar Press Ltd.

Jacobson, K. C. & Crockett, L. J. (2000). Parental monitoring and adolescent adjustment: An ecological perspective. *Journal of Research on Adolescence*, *10*(1), 65–97.

Janssens, K. A., Oldehinkel, A. J. & Rosmalen, J. G. (2009). Parental overprotection predicts the development of functional somatic symptoms in young adolescents. *Journal of Pediatrics*, *154*(6), 918–923.

Kakihara, F., Tilton-Weaver, L., Kerr, M. & Stattin, H. (2010). The relationship of parental control to youth adjustment: Do youths' feelings about their parents play a role? *Journal of Youth and Adolescence*, *39*(12), 1442–1456.

Keijsers, L., Frijns, T., Branje, S. J. & Meeus, W. (2009). Developmental links of adolescent disclosure, parental solicitation, and control with delinquency: Moderation by parental support. *Developmental Psychology*, *45*(5), 1314.

Keijsers, L. & Laird, R. D. (2014). Mother–adolescent monitoring dynamics and the legitimacy of parental authority. *Journal of Adolescence*, *37*(5), 515–524.

Kerr, M. & Stattin, H. (2000). What parents know, how they know it, and several forms of adolescent adjustment: Further support for a reinterpretation of monitoring. *Developmental Psychology*, *36*(3), 366.

Kerr, M. & Stattin, H. (2003). Parenting of adolescence: Action or reaction? In A. C. Crouter & A. Booth (Eds.), *Children's Influence on Family Dynamics: The neglected side of family relationships* (pp. 121–151). Mahwah, NJ: Lawrence Erlbaum.

Kerr, M., Stattin, H. & Burk, W. J. (2010). A reinterpretation of parental monitoring in longitudinal perspective. *Journal of Research on Adolescence*, *20*(1), 39–64.

Kerr, M., Stattin, H. & Pakalniskiene, V. (2008). Parents react to adolescent problem behaviors by worrying more and monitoring less. In M. Kerr, H. Stattin & C. M. E. Rutger (Eds.), *What Can Parents Do?: New insights into the role of parents in adolescent problem behavior* (pp. 91–112). Hoboken, NJ: John Wiley & Sons.

Kilgore, K., Snyder, J. & Lentz, C. (2000). The contribution of parental discipline, parental monitoring, and school risk to early-onset conduct problems in African American boys and girls. *Developmental Psychology*, *36*(6), 835.

Kochanska, G. & Aksan, N. (2006). Children's conscience and self-regulation. *Journal of Personality*, *74*(6), 1587–1618.

Kuhn, T. S. (1970). *The Structure of Scientific Revolutions*. Chicago: University of Chicago Press.

Laird, R. D., Marrero, M. D., Melching, J. A. & Kuhn, E. S. (2013). Information management strategies in early adolescence: Developmental change in use and transactional associations with psychological adjustment. *Developmental Psychology*, *49*(5), 928.

Laird, R. D., Marrero, M. D. & Sentse, M. (2010). Revisiting parental monitoring: Evidence that parental solicitation can be effective when needed most. *Journal of Youth and Adolescence*, *39*(12), 1431–1441.

Laird, R. D., Pettit, G. S., Bates, J. E. & Dodge, K. A. (2003). Parents' monitoring-relevant knowledge and adolescents' delinquent behavior: Evidence of correlated developmental changes and reciprocal influences. *Child Development*, *74*(3), 752–768.

Lahey, B. B., Van Hulle, C. A., D'Onofrio, B. M., Rodgers, J. L. & Waldman, I. D. (2008). Is parental knowledge of their adolescent offspring's whereabouts and peer associations spuriously associated with offspring delinquency? *Journal of Abnormal Child Psychology*, 36(6), 807–823.

Lavi-Levavi, I., Shachar, I. & Omer, H. (2013). Training in nonviolent resistance for parents of violent children: Differences between fathers and mothers. *Journal of Systemic Therapies*, 32(4), 79–93.

LeMoyne, T. & Buchanan, T. (2011). Does "hovering" matter? Helicopter parenting and its effect on well-being. *Sociological Spectrum*, 31(4), 399–418.

Levy, D. M. (1943). *Maternal Overprotection*. New York: Columbia University Press.

Li, X., Feigelman, S. & Stanton, B. (2000). Perceived parental monitoring and health risk behaviors among urban low-income African-American children and adolescents. *Journal of Adolescent Health*, 27(1), 43–48.

Lippold, M. A., Greenberg, M. T. & Collins, L. M. (2013). Parental knowledge and youth risky behavior: A person-oriented approach. *Journal of Youth and Adolescence*, 42(11), 1732–1744.

Lippold, M. A., Greenberg, M. T. & Collins, L. M. (2014). Youths' substance use and changes in parental knowledge-related behaviors during middle school: A person-oriented approach. *Journal of Youth and Adolescence*, 43(5), 729–744.

Lochman, J. E. & van den Steenhoven, A. (2002). Family-based approaches to substance abuse prevention. *Journal of Primary Prevention*, 23(1), 49–114.

Magoon, M. E. & Ingersoll, G. M. (2006). Parental modeling, attachment, and supervision as moderators of adolescent gambling. *Journal of Gambling Studies*, 22(1), 1–22.

Marshall, S. K., Tilton-Weaver, L. C. & Bosdet, L. (2005). Information management: Considering adolescents' regulation of parental knowledge. *Journal of Adolescence*, 28(5), 633–647.

Montgomery, N. (2010). *The negative impact of helicopter parenting on personality*. Poster session presented at the Annual Meeting of the Association of Psychological Science, Boston, MA.

Mullins, L. L., Wolfe-Christensen, C., Pai, A. L. H., Carpentier, M. Y., Gillaspy, S., Cheek, J. & Page, M. (2007). The relationship of parental overprotection, perceived child vulnerability, and parenting stress to uncertainty in youth with chronic illness. *Journal of Pediatric Psychology*, 32(8), 973–982.

Munich, R. L. & Munich, M. A. (2009). Overparenting and the narcissistic pursuit of attachment. *Psychiatric Annals*, 39, 227–235.

Newman, M., Fagan, C. & Webb, R. (2014). Innovations in practice: The efficacy of nonviolent resistance groups in treating aggressive and controlling children and young people: A preliminary analysis of pilot NVR groups in Kent. *Child and Adolescent Mental Health*, 19(2), 138–141.

Nucci, L. P. (2001). *Education in the Moral Domain*. London: Cambridge University Press.

Ollefs, B., Schlippe, A. V., Omer, H. & Kriz, J. (2009). Youngsters with externalizing behavior problems: Effects of parent training (published in German). *Familiendynamik*, 34, 256–265.

Omer, H. (2004). *Nonviolent Resistance: A New Approach to Violent and Self-Destructive Children*. London: Cambridge University Press.

Omer, H. (2015). *Vigilant Care: How parents become a good anchor to their children* (published in German). Göttingen: Vandenhoeck & Ruprecht.

Omer, H., Guttman-Steinmetz, S. G., Carthy, T. & von Schlippe, A. (2013). The anchoring function: Parental authority and the parent-child bond. *Family Process*, *52*(2), 193–206.

Overbeek, G., ten Have, M., Vollebergh, W. & de Graaf, R. (2007). Parental lack of care and overprotection. *Social Psychiatry and Psychiatric Epidemiology*, *42*(2), 87–93.

Padilla-Walker, L. M. & Nelson, L. J. (2012). Black hawk down?: Establishing helicopter parenting as a distinct construct from other forms of parental control during emerging adulthood. *Journal of Adolescence*, *35*(5), 1177–1190.

Padilla-Walker, L. M., Nelson, L. J. & Knapp, D. J. (2014). "Because I'm still the parent, that's why!" Parental legitimate authority during emerging adulthood. *Journal of Social and Personal Relationships*, *31*(3), 293–313.

Pardini, D. A. (2008). Novel insights into longstanding theories of bidirectional parent-child influences: Introduction to the special section. *Journal of Abnormal Child Psychology*, *36*(5), 627–631.

Parker, G. & Lipscombe, P. (1981). Influences of maternal overprotection. *British Journal of Psychiatry*, *138*(4), 303–311.

Pettit, G. S. & Laird, R. D. (2002). Psychological control and monitoring in early adolescence: The role of parental involvement and earlier child adjustment. B. K. Barber (Ed.), *Intrusive Parenting: How psychological control affects children and adolescents* (pp. 97–123). Washington, DC: American Psychological Association.

Pettit, G. S., Laird, R. D., Dodge, K. A., Bates, J. E. & Criss, M. M. (2001). Antecedents and behavior-problem outcomes of parental monitoring and psychological control in early adolescence. *Child Development*, *72*(2), 583–598.

Plunkett, S. W. & Bámaca-Gómez, M. Y. (2003). The relationship between parenting, acculturation, and adolescent academics in Mexican-origin immigrant families in Los Angeles. *Hispanic Journal of Behavioral Sciences*, *25*(2), 222–239.

Racz, S. J. & McMahon, R. J. (2011). The relationship between parental knowledge and monitoring and child and adolescent conduct problems: A 10-year update. *Clinical Child and Family Psychology Review*, *14*(4), 377–398.

Rai, A. A., Stanton, B., Wu, Y., Li, X., Galbraith, J., Cottrell, L., Pack, R., Harris, C., D'Alessandri, D. & Burns, J. (2003). Relative influences of perceived parental monitoring and perceived peer involvement on adolescent risk behaviors: An analysis of six cross-sectional data sets. *Journal of Adolescent Health*, *33*(2), 108–118.

Ramirez, J. R., Crano, W. D., Quist, R., Burgoon, M., Alvaro, E. M. & Grandpre, J. (2004). Acculturation, familism, parental monitoring, and knowledge as predictors of marijuana and inhalant use in adolescents. *Psychology of Addictive Behaviors*, *18*(1), 3.

Rodgers-Farmer, A. Y. (2001). Parental monitoring and peer group association: Their influence on adolescent substance use. *Journal of Social Service Research*, *27*(2), 1–18.

Rote, W. M. & Smetana, J. G. (2015). Beliefs about parents' right to know: Domain differences and associations with change in concealment. *Journal of Research on Adolescence*. Advance online publication. doi:10.1111/jora.12194

Ryan, R. M. & Deci, E. L. (2000). Self-determination theory and the facilitation of intrinsic motivation, social development, and well-being. *American Psychologist*, *55*(1), 68.

Segrin, C., Woszidlo, A., Givertz, M., Bauer, A. & Taylor Murphy, M. (2012). The association between overparenting, parent–child communication, and entitlement and adaptive traits in adult children. *Family Relations*, *61*(2), 237–252.

Segrin, C., Woszidlo, A., Givertz, M. & Montgomery, N. (2013). Parent and child traits associated with overparenting. *Journal of Social and Clinical Psychology*, *32*(6), 569–595.

Shimshoni, Y., Farah, H., Lotan, T., Grimberg, E., Dritter, O., Musicant, O., Toledo, T. & Omer, H. (2015). Effects of parental vigilant care and feedback on novice driver risk. *Journal of Adolescence*, *38*, 69–80.

Shoup, R., Gonyea, R. M. & Kuh, G. D. (2009, June). Helicopter parents: Examining the impact of highly involved parents on student engagement and educational outcomes. Paper presented at the 49th Annual Forum of the Association for Institutional Research, Atlanta, GA. Retrieved from http://cpr.iub.edu/uploads/AIR.

Smetana, J. G. & Daddis, C. (2002). Domain-specific antecedents of parental psychological control and monitoring: The role of parenting beliefs and practices. *Child Development*, *73*(2), 563–580.

Smetana, J. G. & Metzger, A. (2008). Don't ask, don't tell (your mom and dad): Disclosure and nondisclosure in adolescent-parent relationships. In M. Kerr, H. Stattin & C. M. E. Rutger (Eds.), *What Can Parents Do?: New insights into the role of parents in adolescent problem behavior* (pp. 65–87). Hoboken, NJ: John Wiley & Sons.

Smetana, J. G., Metzger, A., Gettman, D. C. & Campione-Barr, N. (2006). Disclosure and secrecy in adolescent–parent relationships. *Child Development*, *77*(1), 201–217.

Smetana, J. G., Villalobos, M., Tasopoulos-Chan, M., Gettman, D. C. & Campione-Barr, N. (2009). Early and middle adolescents' disclosure to parents about activities in different domains. *Journal of Adolescence*, *32*(3), 693–713.

Soenens, B. & Vansteenkiste, M. (2010). A theoretical upgrade of the concept of parental psychological control: Proposing new insights on the basis of self-determination theory. *Developmental Review*, *30*(1), 74–99.

Soenens, B., Vansteenkiste, M., Luyckx, K. & Goossens, L. (2006). Parenting and adolescent problem behavior: An integrated model with adolescent self-disclosure and perceived parental knowledge as intervening variables. *Developmental Psychology*, *42*(2), 305.

Soenens, B., Vansteenkiste, M. & Niemiec, C. P. (2009). Should parental prohibition of adolescents' peer relationships be prohibited? *Personal Relationships*, *16*(4), 507–530.

Soenens, B., Vansteenkiste, M. & Luyten, P. (2010). Toward a domain-specific approach to the study of parental psychological control: Distinguishing between dependency-oriented and achievement-oriented psychological control. *Journal of Personality*, *78*(1), 217–256.

Sorbring, E. & Lundin, L. (2012). Mothers' and fathers' insights into teenagers' use of the internet. *New Media & Society*, *14*(7), 1181–1197.

Spokas, M. & Heimberg, R. G. (2009). Overprotective parenting, social anxiety, and external locus of control: Cross-sectional and longitudinal relationships. *Cognitive Therapy and Research*, *33*(6), 543–551.

Stattin, H. & Kerr, M. (2000). Parental monitoring: A reinterpretation. *Child Development*, *71*(4), 1072–1085.

Stattin, H., Kerr, M. & Tilton-Weaver, L. (2010). Parental monitoring: A critical examination of the research. In V. Guilamo-Ramos, J. Jaccard & P. Dittus (Eds.), *Parental Monitoring of Adolescents: Current perspectives for researchers and practitioners*. New York: Columbia University Press.

Steeves, V. & Webster, C. (2007). Closing the barn door: The effect of parental supervision on Canadian children's online privacy. *Bulletin of Science, Technology & Society*, *21*(1), 4–19.

Steinberg, L. (2005). Psychological control: Style or substance? *New Directions for Child and Adolescent Development*, 2005(108), 71–78.

Stone, L. L., Otten, R., Janssens, J. M., Soenens, B., Kuntsche, E. & Engels, R. C. (2013). Does parental psychological control relate to internalizing and externalizing problems in early childhood? An examination using the Berkeley puppet interview. *International Journal of Behavioral Development*, 37(4), 309–318.

Thomasgard, M. (1998). Parental perceptions of child vulnerability, overprotection, and parental psychological characteristics. *Child Psychiatry and Human Development*, 28(4), 223–240.

Thomasgard, M. & Metz, W. P. (1993). Parental overprotection revisited. *Child Psychiatry and Human Development*, 24(2), 67–80.

Thomasgard, M. & Metz, W. P. (1997). Parental overprotection and its relation to perceived child vulnerability. *American Journal of Orthopsychiatry*, 67(2), 330.

Tilton-Weaver, L. (2014). Adolescents' information management: Comparing ideas about why adolescents disclose to or keep secrets from their parents. *Journal of Youth and Adolescence*, 43(5), 803–813.

Tilton-Weaver, L., Kerr, M., Pakalniskeine, V., Tokic, A., Salihovic, S. & Stattin, H. (2010). Open up or close down: How do parental reactions affect youth information management? *Journal of Adolescence*, 33(2), 333–346.

Toney, L. P., Kelley, M. L. & Lanclos, N. F. (2003). Self-and parental monitoring of homework in adolescents: Comparative effects on parents' perceptions of homework behavior problems. *Child & Family Behavior Therapy*, 25(1), 35–51.

Ungar, M. (2009). Overprotective parenting: Helping parents provide children the right amount of risk and responsibility. *American Journal of Family Therapy*, 37(3), 258–271.

Vitaro, F., Brendgen, M. & Tremblay, R. E. (2001). Preventive intervention: Assessing its effects on the trajectories of delinquency and testing for mediational processes. *Applied Developmental Science*, 5(4), 201–213.

Waizenhofer, R. N., Buchanan, C. M. & Jackson-Newsom, J. (2004). Mothers' and fathers' knowledge of adolescents' daily activities: Its sources and its links with adolescent adjustment. *Journal of Family Psychology*, 18(2), 348.

Wang, Q., Pomerantz, E. M. & Chen, H. (2007). The role of parents' control in early adolescents' psychological functioning: A longitudinal investigation in the United States and China. *Child Development*, 78(5), 1592–1610.

Wartman, K. L. & Savage, M. (2008). *Parental Involvement in Higher Education: Understanding the relationship among students, parents, and the institution*. San Francisco: Jossey-Bass.

Weinblatt, U. & Omer, H. (2008). Nonviolent resistance: A treatment for parents of children with acute behavior problems. *Journal of Marital and Family Therapy*, 34(1), 75–92.

Wilder, E. I. & Watt, T. T. (2002). Risky parental behavior and adolescent sexual activity at first coitus. *Milbank Quarterly*, 80(3), 481–524.

Willoughby, T. & Hamza, C. A. (2011). A longitudinal examination of the bidirectional associations among perceived parenting behaviors, adolescent disclosure and problem behavior across the high school years. *Journal of Youth and Adolescence*, 40(4), 463–478.

Willoughby, B. J., Hersh, J. N., Padilla-Walker, L. M. & Nelson, L. J. (2013). "Back off"! Helicopter parenting and a retreat from marriage among emerging adults. *Journal of Family Issues*, 36(5), 669–692.

Wood, J. J. (2006). Parental intrusiveness and children's separation anxiety in a clinical sample. *Child Psychiatry and Human Development*, 37(1), 73–87.

Wood, M. D., Read, J. P., Mitchell, R. E. & Brand, N. H. (2004). Do parents still matter? Parent and peer influences on alcohol involvement among recent high school graduates. *Psychology of Addictive Behaviors*, *18*(1), 19.

Wright, J. P. & Cullen, F. T. (2001). Parental efficacy and delinquent behavior: Do control and support matter? *Criminology*, *39*(3), 677–706.

2 Vigilant Care in Daily Life

with Tal Fisher and Shai Satran

Families who do things together afford their children a sense of security. A number of studies have shown that children in families who regularly eat meals together are at reduced risk of dropping out of school, substance abuse, associating with a bad crowd, depression and suicidal ideation (for example: Fiese & Schwartz, 2008; Fulkerson, Kubik, Story, Lytle & Arcan, 2009; Han & Fox, 2011). Just as breast milk inoculates the baby against illness, family dinners and other joint family activities seem to inoculate children against other risks. The protective effect of family dinners is probably due to the fact that they allow for close contact between parent and child, and convey feelings of safety and belonging. Family dinners and other family activities serve as an anchor, allowing the child to feel grounded and connected.

The everyday relationship with a child is different from the focused attention that is required when warning signals are detected. When signs of danger appear, we focus on the threat. This is different from our usual openness to whatever is happening around us. A mindset of open attention, which can be comfortably maintained during family dinners and other joint activities, may be so spontaneous that it appears almost totally passive. In fact, the opposite is true: open attention actually represents an active, broad and continuous presence that allows parents to notice positive as well as problematic events, providing the child with a sense of constant accompaniment. This kind of unobtrusive parental activity became clear in a study in which we interviewed 30 parents about their approaches to looking after their children (Fisher, 2013). The quotes in this chapter are derived from that study.

Family activities and other routine contacts between parents and child provide a guarantee that in the moment of truth—when the parents are confronted with danger signals—they will be able to intensify their involvement in an appropriate way. Thus, the steps by which parents exercise an open and non-intrusive attention set the stage for focused and decided action when needed.

Routine Contact

Countless random and planned daily contacts allow parents to get a good picture of their child's situation, while conveying messages of closeness and guidance.

> I pick up the girls from school twice a week. I've noticed that on those days, they spontaneously give me a vivid description of the day's events: how was math class, what happened in recess, who fought with whom. However, on the days when I meet the girls later in the afternoon, they give a more generic account of their experiences and only if I ask specific questions.
>
> My husband helped our son with a presentation before a class trip and I helped him organize a party for his friends. That is our way of knowing what happens at these events: Once you've helped, you have the right to ask questions!
>
> Our son was always glad to go visit Grandma and Grandpa. All of a sudden he started avoiding those visits, and when he did come, he would sit in the car sullen and withdrawn. Eventually, I realized this had to do with his going out the night before. He had new friends and on Fridays he came home pretty late. When he woke up in the morning, he was still under the influence of the night's events. We understood that we were entering a new phase.

A parent who manages to maintain daily contacts with his child will find it easier to notice any changes. He has a point of reference. The constant meetings are like a net of sensors, sensitive to any deviation.

Routine contact does more than just contribute to parental knowledge. It also strengthens the parents' presence in the child's mind. Thus, the child's schedule includes not only school, extracurricular activities and friends, but also contacts with his parents. This background of parental presence fosters the development of self-care. A child who is about to meet with a parent will cope with temptations better than a child who feels disconnected. She will feel accompanied by a parental presence in her own mind, which helps her control herself in different situations. This is probably one of the reasons why family dinners are beneficial. The fact that the child can expect an upcoming family meal, or has an aftertaste of a recent one, acts as a reminder: "My parents are close by, my family is close, my home is close."

> When my daughter goes out to a party, I always prefer to drive her there or back so that when she's at the party, she keeps me in mind. I also arrange to have another parent drive her the other way.

Increasing the frequency of daily contacts is a good way for parents to broaden their vigilant care. Many parents wonder how they can do so after the child is already used to having almost limitless freedom of movement and minimal contact with them. The answer, as in many similar situations, has to do with their sense of legitimacy. When a parent clearly feels this is her duty, she will be able to increase her presence without hesitation.

Parents of adolescents often feel that they need their child's consent to increase their involvement. This assumption makes it difficult for parents to intensify their vigilance, even when this is clearly required. Other parents try to cope with this difficulty by having recourse to an implicit kind of supervision, or even to downright spying. However, parents must understand that vigilant care is an essential part of their parental duty, and their child cannot veto it. Children should know that their parents are always attentive to what is happening to them. Without this awareness, they will miss the essential experience of parental accompaniment, which is probably a major factor in the development of self-care. Vigilant care is therefore most effective when the parent has the courage to be open about it.

> The father of a 13-year-old drove his son to his first nighttime outing with friends. "I want to drive you so I can make sure you arrive well, and to know where you are spending your time!"

The father openly asserted his duty and justified his action. That would not have happened if the father had found an excuse to explain why he was driving his son to the meeting place. When practiced openly, vigilant care conveys the message, "Whatever happens to you is my concern!"

The Network of Vigilant Care

Parents who try to exercise vigilant care on their own will quickly discover that they are limited in their ability to perceive warning signs and take action. Those parents are then more at a risk of acting invasively or covertly when troubles arise. The situation is wholly different when they succeed in building a network of support, including other family members, teachers and parents of their child's friends. Support allows the parents to develop a set of broader and more sensitive sensors. At the same time, it provides the child with a potentially caring and protective net.

Some parents tend to avoid addressing people outside the nuclear family. They often say: "My daughter will die of shame!" or "I don't want to bother other people!" This line of thought illustrates the privacy reflex, one of whose chief effects is to limit parents' ability to exercise vigilant care. Privacy is an important value in our culture, but making it absolute renders the task of parenting extremely difficult. Parents should therefore match the privacy they accord their child to the degree of responsibility he shows. Thus, a child who endangers himself or uses his privacy negatively loses some of his privacy rights.

The privacy reflex follows the assumption that all shame is bad. There is no doubt that shame is an unpleasant emotion. Many children react strongly when their parents disclose their problems. While this may be embarrassing, it is not necessarily a harmful experience. Harm will only ensue when disclosure is accompanied by disrespect and lack of support. Thus, a child who is humiliated may suffer considerable harm, but a child who experiences shame in a supportive context may be benefited in his development (Weinblatt, 2016). It is therefore vital that any confrontation regarding a problem behavior be made in a respectful and supportive way. This happens, for instance, when the confrontation is accompanied by messages of care and appreciation. In this way, a positive context emerges, modulating the experience of shame, so that rather than feeling alone and outcast, the child may feel supported and upheld. For instance, saying to a child "Your self-respect is very important to me!" may allow the child to overcome the shame of exposure. Interestingly, by saying to a child that we respect him, we actually give him respect. For this reason, affirming the child's self-respect may change the shameful exposure into a meaningful experience.

The understanding that experiences of shame in a supportive context are important to development is growing. Violent youth have been characterized by an inability to cope with shame because they never experienced shame in a supportive context (Findeisen & Kersten, 1999). In recent years, a number of programs have been developed to counter youth delinquency within a framework of *restorative justice* that actually provide experiences in "restorative shame." Those programs are based on the assumption that shame that is experienced in a respectful context can have very positive consequences (Palermo, 2013). As part of such programs, the delinquent meets with his victim, along with members of both families. During such a meeting, the delinquent faces the consequences of his actions to the victim and the victim's family, but he is also afforded the opportunity to do emotional and material reparation. While restorative justice, with its elaborate demands, is probably only applicable to a small percentage of cases, the use of supporters can have similar results without requiring excessive investment. In our opinion, the judicious use of a support network is enough to create the positive context that allows for the experience of restorative shame. Our findings support this hypothesis: our treatment protocol for violent and self-destructive kids, which is largely based on the parents' support network, has been found to significantly reduce child violence and risk behaviors (Omer & Lebowitz, 2016).

It is important to understand that the restriction of privacy rights is not a punishment, but an action that is necessary for the child's safety. The child can be expected to resist the parents' attempts to reduce his privacy, but when those measures are legitimized by the supporters, his resistance wanes. The message "Your parents cannot give you up! Neither can we!" often has a powerful impact. Some adolescents later confide that they felt relieved when their previous harmful privacy gave way to a protective network. Instead of drifting into the open sea on their own, they began feeling anchored and attached.

Cooperation Between Parents

Parents can cooperate even when they don't think alike. In fact, the attempt to pressure one's spouse into accepting one's point of view is often a major obstacle to cooperation, as people tend to resist efforts to change their minds, especially when they're in conflict. This understanding allows couples to begin looking after their child better, even when they disagree in many other matters. Sometimes all that can be achieved, at least initially, is a very partial cooperation, such as agreeing on major goals, or even less—agreeing not to sabotage one another's efforts. Other couples succeed in agreeing on a plan of vigilant care, thus creating a more positive scenario for risk reduction.

> Simon and Drea were worried that Eli (14) was spending more and more time closed up in his room with the computer. Sometimes he sat in front of the screen until dawn. After talking it over they decided to give Eli a joint message. They entered his room together, asked him to stop playing with the computer for a minute, and then told him: "We don't accept that you spend so many hours at the computer, and especially late at night. We decided on a new rule: The computer will be turned off at 22:00. We will make sure this happens!"

If, on the following days, the parents take turns ensuring that the computer is off at the stipulated time, the intervention will probably be successful. This kind of cooperation is especially important when new rules are formulated. When there is already a basic agreement, the parents can also act on their own, if the matter at hand is not especially grave. Even then, however, notifying the other is a good idea, especially when the other parent is willing to tell the child that he has been notified and agrees:

> Dora discovered that Neil (13) had been neglecting his homework, and that he not only hid his F in English but didn't even let her know there was an exam. Usually she was the one who was responsible for supervising Neil's schooling. Her husband Patrick worked late and contact with his son was limited to the weekend. Dora didn't feel she had to involve Patrick intensively, but she shared their son's school problem with him. She asked him to let Neil know that he was aware of his concealment and agreed with Dora in her decision to supervise his schoolwork closely.

Though in this example the mother is the one doing the actual work, her position is strengthened by her husband's support. Unfortunately, even this modest level of cooperation is not always obtainable. The goal can then be even more modest: asking the other parent not to sabotage the intervention. Surprisingly, even this low level of cooperation can prove significant, particularly if the marginal parent is updated in a respectful manner.

> George and Lina had been divorced for ten years. For a good part of that time, Lina had lived abroad with their two daughters. During those years, George's involvement in the girls' lives diminished considerably. Lina avoided contact with George and minimized his part in her decisions regarding the children. When the mother and daughters returned from abroad, the girls began visiting their father about once a month. At this time, Jessica (15) began going out with friends, sometimes vanishing for many hours and coming back in the middle of the night. Lina went to a counselor to get help on how to cope with the problem. The counselor phoned George and asked him if he was willing to participate. George replied he would not take part in the counseling. The counselor accepted his reservations, but asked him if he could come to only one session, so as to know what was going on and be told about the measures that were being planned to deal with his daughter's disappearances. George agreed to come. The counselor told him that his wish not to take part in the counseling would be respected. He was then presented with the problems that had brought Lina to the program and with the plan for stepping up Lina's level of vigilant care. The counselor then asked for George's permission to send him short written updates concerning Jessica's situation and Lina's supervision. George agreed and, to Lina's surprise, said that if there was a special need, he would agree to come to an additional meeting. Furthermore, he told Jessica that he had met with Lina and the counselor and that he agreed with Lina's decisions regarding her behavior.

Even very marginal parents should be updated about their child's situation and the steps being undertaken to deal with it. If the reports are free of demands or accusations, there is a reasonable chance that a positive response may ensue. The following is an example of an update that a divorced mother sent to a very passive and depressed father:

> "Hello Michael, I've decided to periodically share with you the things that concern me and also the things that I'm pleased about in Zoe's behavior. I wanted you to know that she has gotten better at school, especially since her teacher and I decided to check her homework every day. This has also reduced her school absenteeism. I get reports from the teacher and then talk

with Zoe in the evening. She thus knows that I know. I thought it would be good for you to know too. I also want to tell you that I respect your wish not to get involved in ways that caused you pain in the past. But I feel like I should tell you about her, because you are her father and deserve to know. Best, Ruth"

Although there is no expectation that the father undertake any specific action, it is possible that when he meets with his daughter, he may mention the mother's reports. Such acknowledgment can be meaningful, making the world the girl lives in more continuous and less chaotic. Even such a modest sign of cooperation conveys some sense of parental presence to the child.

Support from Outside the Nuclear Family

Grandparents and other relatives are valuable resources in the attempt to reduce risk behaviors of children and adolescents. Research has shown that in families where grandparents or other supporters are involved, the risk of delinquency or drug use is significantly reduced (Dornbusch et al., 1985; Steinberg, 2001). Strengthening the bonds between grandparents and the core family, involving them in the children's problems and increasing the frequency of contacts with them, creates better conditions for vigilant care. In our experience, even grandparents who live far away, or are coping with the hardships of aging, can provide meaningful support. Far from feeling burdened, they feel respected and meaningful to the family.

> Clara and Zach were worried about Alex's (15) withdrawal. He spent more and more time in front of the television and the computer and avoided social contacts. The grandparents, who lived an hour by bus from the family house, were unaware of the situation. Initially, the parents wanted to spare them the worry, as the grandfather was ill and the grandmother exhausted from caring for her husband continuously. With the counselor's encouragement, the parents decided to share their worries with the grandparents. The parents returned late from work, so Alex spent many hours idle and alone. The grandparents reacted positively to the parents' call for help. At first Alex reacted gruffly to his grandparents' phone calls that interrupted the soap operas he had become addicted to. However, he changed his mind after his grandpa started to arrive in person to stay with him. The grandmother called Alex and told him that the wish to help him had filled her husband with energy, so Alex could now feel he was both helper and helped. Gradually a routine of contacts developed: Alex began visiting his

grandfather once a week after school, and the grandfather revived an old tradition they had of watching soccer matches together. This, however, was a different way of watching television: it was a shared activity that helped cement a valuable relationship.

Updating grandparents on the child's doings, both positive and negative, may be a good way to get them back in the picture. If the parents are concerned that one of the grandparents may fall into unhelpful moralizing, he can be specifically asked not to do so. In any case, it is better to have a grandpa who moralizes than one who does not know what is going on.

Involving other family members, as well as close friends of the parents, can have similar effects. It strengthens vigilant care and the child's sense of belonging. The parents break out of their isolation and operate in a wider network that validates their actions and creates a bridge between the home and the outside world.

School personnel can also enrich the parents' ability to exercise vigilant care. Parents who maintain good contacts with the school are more present and informed, while parent–teacher clashes harm vigilant care considerably. The situation is similar with regard to the child's social life. Thus, parents who contact other parents in the child's social circle will be more able to detect signs of trouble and intervene when necessary.

Parents can initiate contact with the parent of a friend at a special event—for example, a field trip, a PTA meeting, a neighborhood party, etc. On being acquainted, the parent can say: "I'd be happy if we could talk more often, so we can update each other on our children. Is that alright with you?" These contacts should also be made known to the child. A parent who feels that this contrasts too much with her past behavior can say to the child: "I have decided to share opinions with other parents. I now understand that it is important for parents to be in touch with one another."

Family friends can add an important layer to the process of vigilant care. Some may have a special connection to the child, which may contribute to a better dialogue. Most parents, however, are not used to asking for help with the tasks of vigilant care, despite considerable benefits. For instance, a close family friend may tell the child: "I heard from your father that you came home in a bad mood after going out with your friends. I'd be happy to help if you'd like. And if you want me to keep certain things between us, I'll respect your wish." The friend is not spying on the parents' behalf. She is assisting them in creating a protective net. This network has room for areas of privacy, without harming the process of vigilant care. In effect, the parents must be close by, but they do not have to know everything. Vigilant care does not invalidate privacy rights, unless privacy is used as a screen to conceal negative behaviors.

Talking with the Child

A central, but often elusive, aspect of vigilant care is the ability to conduct an open talk with the child. What is the secret that allows some parents to foster openness and others not? How can we create an atmosphere in which the child is willing to talk and listen? Many think that this ability is wholly natural and cannot be learned. True, there are parents, or rather parent–child dyads, for whom this kind of contact is totally spontaneous. But that is not the case for all, or even most, parents. Many parents have a hard time establishing a constructive dialogue, especially when discussing topics that are central to vigilant care. The following considerations may improve parents' ability to do so.

The Preacher and the Friend: Two Problematic Poles

A common parental dilemma has to do with the best approach to furthering fruitful discussions. Some parents prefer a conversation between equals, so as to elicit spontaneous disclosure. Others feel they must make their demands and expectations clear to the child. Both positions are justified, but both have their pitfalls. Parents who value openness above all may find it harder to voice their values and experience. On the other hand, parents who warn and preach may prevent disclosure.

> Rebecca, a divorced single mother to Laura (17), aimed at an equal relationship with her daughter. She believed that only a fully open, non-judgmental stance would gain Laura's trust and preserve their close friendship, which in her opinion was the gist of her motherhood. Over the years, she had become her daughter's confidant, and as Laura grew older, she also shared her own secrets with her. One day, Laura confided to her mother that she was engaged in a romantic and sexual relationship with two boys simultaneously. Rebecca was taken aback, but was afraid that voicing her opinion would hurt the trust between them. When she feebly tried to take a stand, Laura threatened never to confide in her again. Rebecca felt she had no choice but to return to a purely non-judgmental position, but she began worrying this might hurt her motherly function.

> Irvin's (13) father, Igor, talked jokingly with his son about smoking with friends. He hoped this would bring his son to open up. Encouraged by the trustful atmosphere, Irvin told him that he sometimes smoked with a friend. At this point, Igor changed his tone and began lecturing his son on the dangers of smoking, and threatened to cut his allowance if Irvin touched a cigarette again. Irvin decided that in the future he should keep this kind of thing to himself.

Accessibility, Openness and Self-Control

Many parents tell their children: "If you have a problem, trust me and I will do everything to help you!" Some children will, in effect, turn to the parent if they have a problem, but others won't, perhaps because they feel they will not really be listened to. Interestingly, most parents we interviewed knew quite well how they prevented their child's openness. When asked why their child avoided coming to them for help, they said: "Because she's afraid I'll get angry!" Learning to control their reactions may help them deal better with those situations. Listening without erupting into preaching or threatening does not invalidate their parental position. On the contrary, by improving their self-control, those parents may remain attuned and give the child a feeling of presence. The fact that they don't scold or protest does not mean they are passive. They can convey their position clearly with their concerned tone and by what comes later in the conversation. Such a controlled reaction allows the child to feel close and cared for in ways that strengthen her in the face of temptation.

> Frank, the father of Ollie (16), said to his son: "If you get in trouble again, come and tell me. I promise I won't be mad or lecture. We will sit down and look for a solution together. And to make sure, remind me that I promised." Ollie took that as a cue and said: "Dad, I have a problem that I want to talk with you about! But please remember what you promised!"
>
> Moses, a divorced father who has joint custody with his ex-wife, noticed that Hank (15) was in a bad mood. Moses was the strict parent and Eva the lenient one. Moses knew that Hank feared his reactions and often tried to hide his problems from him. To improve this situation, he said to Hank: "I can see that something is weighing on you. In the past I have often been impatient and strict. I promise that if you tell me what is going on I will make every effort to react differently and do my best to help you." In the following days, Moses called Hank from work a couple of times, telling him: "I just want to keep more contact with you!" Two weeks later, he took his son for a fishing trip. In the evening, Hank told his father that he was in trouble at school because of two friends who were known as trouble makers. He hinted at what kind of trouble he was in, but avoided giving his father more details. In the past, Moses would have scolded him, especially because he had already warned him about those boys. This time, Moses managed to control himself and say to his son: "I'm glad you're telling me about this. Today and tomorrow we are fishing, so we'll postpone the discussion. When we get home, we'll think together how to get out of this predicament!"

The father's behavior shows how a parent can develop the ability to listen openly and create presence at the same time. He showed his son he was attentive to his state of mind and told him he wanted to know what was troubling him. The phone calls from work showed his son that he was continuously on his father's mind. The father also acknowledged his past errors and worked to overcome his tendency to lecture and scold. When the son made a first attempt to open up, he found his father well prepared. Not only was the ability to exercise vigilant care enhanced in the process, but also the father–son relationship.

Inviting a child out is a good way to create the conditions for a good talk, especially when the outings become a regular event. A father said to his son, with whom he went once a month to a restaurant: "For me this is a special time when we can talk calmly about things. I want to tell you that anything that comes up during our outings won't make me angry!" Creating a special situation, where the rules are different, may induce a sense of security. It helps if the parent talks about himself (his past, his job, his plans), but without burdening the child with disclosures unfit for his age. If the child confides events of a worrisome nature, the parent can show that he is worried, but take care to avoid reacting negatively. He can tell the child: "You are telling me some difficult stuff, and I am sure it isn't easy for you. It isn't easy for me either. Let us let it sink in. We'll look for a way to deal with that later, with a clear head." In doing so, the parent serves as a model of self-control and responsibility.

Parents who succeed in implementing the principle that listening and reacting are two separate stages in dealing with a problem will listen attentively and encourage the child's disclosure. The search for a solution may come at a later time. This two-stage approach helps prevent impulsive reactions. In contrast, a parent who reacts to disclosure with shock or anger may lead the child to the conclusion that it was a mistake to open up. Harsh reactions are usually unhelpful, and most parents can train themselves to control them. In our work with parents of children with acute behavior problems, we have shown that even very impulsive parents can learn to control their reactions to some degree (Omer & Lebowitz, 2016).

At the core of parents' ability to create a better dialogue with their child lies the understanding that holding a good conversation may be more important than finding out exactly what happened. In an open dialogue, the parent assumes an interested and not an investigative stance. The interested stance is characterized by non-judgmental listening and commitment to support the child, whereas the investigative stance aims at unearthing the truth, no matter what. Whereas the interested parent is clearly on the child's side, the investigating parent places himself in an adversarial position.

Some parents might object that an open conversation is pointless if the parent fails to get the crucial information. This is not true. Such conversation can serve parental vigilant care by: (a) increasing the parent's presence in the child's mind; (b) increasing the chances that the child will turn to the parent in case of trouble; (c) enhancing the parent's sensitivity to the child's condition; and (d) allowing the parent to express his concerns in a positive way.

Here are some typical openings that parents use to initiate such conversations:

"Lately I've noticed that you've been coming home from school in a bad mood. It is important for me to know what you are going through!"

"Lately I've been feeling that you are reserved or angry with me. It is important for me to know why. Maybe we can find a solution together."

"Facebook has become a central part of your life. I'm not so computer savvy, so what would you think about giving me a tutorial?"

Such invitations convey interest and concern, while also respecting the child's privacy. Even if an open conversation does not ensue immediately, it may occur in the sequel. When the conversation develops, especially when it includes some worrisome disclosure, it is important to give it an honest and positive closure. For instance:

"I'm happy you trusted me. We have to look for a solution. But first let us both calm down. We'll talk about this again tomorrow when our heads are clearer."

"I'm glad you told me that, but it isn't easy for me. Any parent would be worried to hear something like that. I promised not to get mad or lecture, and I will keep that promise. But we aren't done yet. I'll talk to mom, and the three of us will look for a positive solution."

The last example might be surprising, a father announcing that he will share the content of the conversation with the mother. We want to emphasize that also in a private conversation, the parent represents the parental function, that is, both parents. Except for very special disclosures of an intimate nature, the parent's "I" is actually a "We." A parent who creates with his child a bond of secrecy that excludes the other parent harms vigilant care. We suggest that every parent ask herself honestly if she tends to comply with her child's request to keep problematic occurrences from the other parent. This compliance should then be withheld. For instance, a mother who agreed in the past to conceal information from the father, can repair the damage by saying: "In the past I agreed not to tell your father about problems you had in class, but I've realized that was wrong and have decided that, from now on, I will keep him updated." If the child protests that this is a breach of trust, the mother may reply: "Your trust is very important to me, but I can't allow it to come at the price of concealing things from your father!"

Conveying Messages without Arousing Resistance

Communication between parent and child does not always take the form of dialogue. Parents have to state their position clearly, even if unilaterally. In such cases, it is important to understand the difference between transmitting a message and administering a lecture. When lecturing, parents try to inculcate their position in a repetitive and forceful way. This arouses opposition. Children often resist parental attempts to enforce their messages by closing their ears and minds. Some children seem to comply, while mentally dismissing what the parent says. Interestingly, many parents cannot avoid preaching, even when they feel it is futile. This can be avoided, if parents become aware that these exchanges are damaging and, especially, if they have a better alternative.

Effective parental messages are based on the understanding that vigilant care is not control, and that the parents cannot force their values or life experience on the child. However, the parent can make it clear that, though he cannot enforce his position, he is still obliged to be true to it. A good way to start is by announcing a clear rule in a calm and decisive manner, but without repetition. If the child protests, the parent can respond: "You are part of our family!" or "You live in this house!" Emphasizing the child's belonging while at the same time making the rule clear is a powerful combination. This, however, does not make the child's belonging conditional on his obedience. It would be a mistake to say: "Are you part of this family or not?" Such a veiled threat would harm the child's sense of belonging and paradoxically deepen his self-exclusion. It is as if the child answers the parent's rhetorical question by saying to himself: "Not for long!"

The parents' position is strengthened when it is validated by supporters. For instance, a friend of the parents tells the child: "Your parents told me they want to know where you go out every night, and when exactly you are coming back. I want to tell you that I agree with them, it is the duty of parents to act like that!" When the supporter uses expressions like "It is their duty," "They have no choice," or "That is how it is in our family," this highlights the fact that the parental position is not arbitrary, but expresses a shared value. Parents who wish to do their job without any external support inadvertently weaken the legitimacy of their position. Instead of being backed by their network, they resort to harsher tones and repetitive demands, as if to compensate by sheer vocal intensity for the lack of the broad voice of a supportive net that alone could confer social validity to their attitude and acts. No wonder the attempt often miscarries.

Parents' messages reflecting basic values are often unilateral, in the sense that they can be clarified but not debated. One of the reasons for the erosion of parental presence is the common belief of parents that they need the child's consent for their stance and acts. True, cooperation makes the task easier, but parental vigilant care is also feasible without it. In the next chapter, we will describe ways in which parents can cope with the child's resistance. These are situations that do not fall under the category of routine parental activities, which are the focus of the current chapter. However, also with regard to routine vigilant care, it is important that the parents view their position as an outcome of their function and duty as parents, and not as contingent upon the child's approval. The parent can, of course, say to the child "your cooperation is important to me," but in his heart he must be determined to exercise vigilant care even when the child disagrees. This inner resolve imbues parental messages with a cogency that will never be achieved by loudness or repetitiveness.

Building Joint Scenarios

Another kind of parental activity that strengthens vigilant care in daily life is building joint scenarios for potentially problematic situations. This may be prefaced by a remark like the following:

> "I want to talk with you about your upcoming trip with your friends. It's the first time you're going out for three days without any adults. To be on the safe side, I'd like to think with you about different situations you might encounter and about ways to deal with them."
>
> "I want to talk about some concerns I have about Facebook. I'll feel better if we think together about possible complications and see how to avoid them."

Ideally, those joint scenarios would include a description of what is to take place in the planned event (e.g., a party, trip, etc.), a joint exploration of problems that might arise and a discussion of positive ways of coping with them. It is best to focus first of all on a positive description of the event. Early focus on threats and concerns tends to block cooperation. If the child says, "Enough, Mom, there's nothing to worry about!" the mother can answer, "So let's put aside my worries for a moment. Let's see how this party can be the best possible party!" Focusing first on the positive scenario allows the conversation to unfold without blocking the child's mind with the parent's "exaggerated concerns." The act of building a scenario can inoculate against negative developments, even when these are not discussed explicitly. But it is often possible to add a layer to the positive scenario by saying, "I hope that everything will be fine, and there are good chances that it will be so. Still, I want to ask you how you would react if problems arose." The parent can then refer to some possible problem scenarios: "What will you do if someone offers you a joint?" "What will you do if there is alcohol at the party?" "Who are you coming home with?" Raising those issues one at a time—it is important not to bombard the child with a list of parental worries—strengthens parental presence in the child's mind. It is a good idea to end the conversation with a small request: "Please send me a short message before midnight. It will allow me to sleep well." It is hard to say "No!" to a request that is phrased like that. But if the child is adamant, the parent can say: "I trust you and allow you to go out. All I ask for is a short message so I can sleep quietly." If there is still no change, a possible addition would be: "I do not want to go to bed worried. I am expecting a message from you. That way I won't have to call your friends to make sure that everything is OK." Usually this will do the job.

References

Dornbusch, S., Carlsmith, J., Bushwall, S., Ritter, P., Leiderman, H., Hastorf, A. & Gross, R. (1985). Single parents, extended households and the control of adolescents. *Child Development*, *56*, 326–341.

Fiese, B. H. & Schwartz, M. (2008). Reclaiming the family table: Mealtime and child health and wellbeing. *Social Policy Report*, *22*, 3–18.

Findeisen H.V. & Kersten, J. (1999). *The Meaning of Youth Violence* (published in German). Munich: Kunstmann.

Fisher, T. (2013). Routine vigilant care: According to the principles of the new authority approach. Unpublished master's thesis, Tel-Aviv University.

Fulkerson, J. A., Kubik, M. Y., Story, M., Lytle, L. & Arcan, C. (2009). Are there nutritional and other benefits associated with family meals among at-risk youth? *Journal of Adolescent Health*, *45*(4), 389–395.

Fulkerson, J. A., Story, M., Mellin, A., Leffert, N., Neumark-Sztainer, D. & French, S. A. (2006). Family dinner meal frequency and adolescent development: Relationship with developmental assets and high-risk behaviors. *Journal of Adolescent Health*, *39*(3), 337–345.

Han, W. J. & Fox, L. E. (2011). Parental work schedules and children's cognitive trajectories. *Journal of Marriage and Family*, *73*, 962–980.

Omer, H. & Lebowitz, E. R. (2016). Nonviolent resistance: Helping caregivers reduce problematic behaviors in children and adolescents. *Journal of Marital and Family Therapy*. doi:10.1111/jmft.12168.

Palermo, G.B. (2013). Restorative justice: A more understanding and humane approach to offenders. *International Journal of Offender Therapy and Comparative Criminology*, *57*, 1051–1053.

Weinblatt, U. (2016). *Closeness Is Very Close: Overcoming shame and hurt in relationships* (published in German). Göttingen: Vandenhoeck & Ruprecht.

3   When the Child Resists

with Yoel Everett

Exercising vigilant care does not depend on the child's consent. Cooperation helps create a more pleasant atmosphere, and allows for a friendlier and more open form of vigilant care; however, when warning signs appear, parents must intensify the level of vigilant care, even in the face of the child's protests.

Parents often react harshly when they discover their child is involved in harmful activities. Such reactions are mostly instinctive, but they are also fueled by the hope that the child will be daunted enough to stop his problematic behavior at once. Unfortunately, this expectation is often illusory. A negative behavior pattern cannot usually be ended in one stroke. Parents would do better to prepare themselves to exercise a higher level of vigilant care for an extended period. The following comparison clarifies the difference between the unrealistic expectation of shaking the child up through a sharp confrontation and the enduring stance of persistent vigilant care:

Expectations of Immediate Change

The parent expects that a sharp confrontation will put an immediate end to the child's problematic behavior.
The parent amasses evidence to confront the child with his faulty behavior.
The parent threatens or punishes severely.
The parent screams, blames and uses extreme language.
The parent loses her self-control.
When change does not ensue, the parent feels defeated.

Persistent Vigilant Care

The parent remains vigilant for as long as necessary, even when the child protests.
The parent knows that change is usually gradual and sometimes partial.
The parent tells the child that she will look after him closely.
The parent maintains her self-control, even when the child provokes her.
The parent remains committed to vigilant care, even when there are no evident improvements.

Many parents must first experience the failure of the first approach in order to develop the patience and persistence needed for the second. After all, it is only natural to react with indignation upon discovery of offensive and harmful acts. However, when they are already acquainted with the child's problematic behaviors and know that sharp reactions fail to bring the desired result, their approach must change. It helps if they know the probable consequences of continuing with the old approach.

Confrontation and Disconnection

When parents expect immediate change, they direct all their attention to the child's reactions. They expect that if confronted with their anger and shock, the child will show regret, promise to improve and abide by that commitment. Failing this, the parents often try to achieve their goal through dire threats. If the desired change does not ensue, they feel obliged to carry out the threats, in order not to lose credibility. However, most parents find it difficult to enforce the threatened punishment, or find that their child reverts back to his disruptive behavior after "serving his time." The result is usually an increase in the parents' sense of helplessness.

The attempt to force immediate change often makes confrontations more severe. Instead of complying, the child responds in kind, by screaming, cursing and threatening. The price of escalation can be high: the situation deteriorates, the parents become exhausted, and the family becomes accustomed to screams and threats (Patterson, Dishion & Bank, 1984). This process is similar to the way we habituate to a noisy environment by disregarding the usual level of noise and noticing only noise at a higher level. Gradually, the parents become hopeless and exhausted. The mere idea of a new confrontation causes deep reluctance. To avoid this, parents learn to buy quiet, keeping the child at a safe distance and leaving him to himself. Gradually, their view of the child becomes negative and they feel they have failed in their parental role. The relationship between the parents may also be badly affected. For instance, the stricter parent may blame the other for giving in, while the more lenient parent may blame the other for rejecting the child.

The child often feels that giving in to the parents' demands, particularly when presented in the form of an ultimatum, is an unbearable humiliation. To his mind, only two options remain: open defiance or concealing his activities. Many children do both, blatantly challenging their parents, while pursuing their dangerous course in secret. The child's arsenal in this fight is virtually unlimited. It includes provocations and offenses that make the parents lose control; explicit and tacit threats geared to activate the parents' deepest anxieties; and an attitude of indifference and non-responsiveness. The more the parents attempt to shake him up or penetrate his armor, the more entrenched he becomes. Parents and child develop the feeling that they are living in separate worlds, ruled by opposite laws. No wonder they choose to reduce their contacts to a minimum and follow a tacit norm of mutual avoidance.

How Can the Parents Strengthen Their Position?

One of the chief difficulties is that parents tend to focus almost exclusively on the child's behavior. The parental discourse narrows down to an obsessive repetition of the child's acts: "He doesn't give a damn about us!" "She vanishes every night!" "He steals!" "She lies!" This narrow focus has been nicknamed "symptom trance" (Gilligan, 1987). Like a person in a hypnotic trance, whose attention is completely captured by the hypnotist, the parents seem hypnotized by the child, bewitched by his acts, unable to break its spell and regain the initiative.

Parents begin to reassume effective parenting, when they (a) understand that they cannot control the child, but only themselves; and (b) start focusing on their own duty, instead of on the child's misbehaviors. Those processes reinforce each other: when the parents understand that they can only control themselves, they can focus on their parental duty; and when they keep their parental duty in mind, they free themselves from the destructive fight for control that rendered them helpless. For instance:

- It is very difficult to get a child who attacks a sibling out of jealousy to change her feelings. However, the parents can tell her: "We cannot dictate your feelings toward your brother. However, we'll resist any acts of violence or humiliation against him."
- It is very difficult to motivate a child who dislikes studying to do so. However, the parents can tell him: "We cannot force you to be a good student. But it is our duty to check whether you skip classes, take your school material with you and do your homework. From now on, we'll be in daily contact with your teacher about those matters!"
- It is very difficult to convince a temptation-prone adolescent to take care of herself in each and every case. However, the parents can tell her: "We've no control over your acts when you are away. But it's our duty to look after you more closely, particularly after what happened last month!"
- It is very difficult to stop a child's problematic and excessive use of computers. However, the parents can tell their child: "We don't agree to you sitting at the computer late at night. After what happened last week, we want to know what is going on. We'll make visits to your room and check up on you more closely!"

Managing Confrontations

Self-control is a central component of the parents' anchoring function. Many parents find it difficult to invest in the development of self-control, because they think that if they refrain from fighting back with all their might, the child will think they are weak. The expectation that they should control themselves when the child provokes them seems to them preposterous, as it would show the child that she can get away with anything. They feel obliged to win every confrontation. If they don't react, they are losers. Our position is the precise opposite: parental strength is reflected in the ability to persist in one's parental goals without being dragged into provocations or shows of force. Parents who believe they have to show the child who is the boss are only showing their lack of self-assurance.

When parents wish to intensify their vigilant care in the wake of the warning signs they detect, they must be prepared to withstand the child's protests. The child's reactions actually reflect the attempt to shake their determination. She may do this by casting doubt on the legitimacy of their acts, by dragging them into arguments, or by threatening with dire consequences. For instance:

> A 14-year-old girl yelled at her mother after the mother called her friends when she refused to say where she was: "You've destroyed my social life! You've turned me into a laughing stock! Because of you I cannot go back to school!"
>
> A 13-year-old boy who used to steal money from his parents tried to engage his father in an argument, after the father searched his room. The boy repeated again and again that by entering the room in his absence, his father had completely destroyed the trust between them.
>
> A 17-year-old boy threatened his mother, after she had talked with the mother of his 15-year-old girlfriend: "If you ever do this again, you won't see me anymore!"

Usually, the very readiness of the parents to engage in a discussion over such claims may signal that they are not fully determined. We all know that a decision that is under discussion is not final. For this reason, it is important that parents prepare beforehand for this eventuality, so as not to lift the anchor they are trying to cast.

Conveying Decisiveness

Most children react moderately to the parents' attempts to look after them when this is clearly linked to situations of risk (Padilla-Walker, Nelson & Knapp, 2014). Most likely this is because, in addition to their attraction to forbidden thrills, children also have a need for security. Parents who show their child that they will not give up on him and will maintain their presence in his life answer those deep-seated needs. Although the child strives to expand the scope of his autonomy, he is aware of the parents' duty to protect him, and also of his own need for an accompanying presence. However, some children are so averse to parental supervision that they are willing to take their resistance quite far.

Parents often react to the child's screams, threats and extreme acts by giving in or lashing back. Although those are opposite reactions, the result is equally bad. When parents capitulate and stop exercising vigilant care, the child remains at risk and learns that he can get rid of his parents' disturbing presence by aggravating the conflict. When the parents scream back and threaten with dire consequences, the child often concludes: "It's either them or me!" He then feels he has no choice but to fight to the bitter end or act in secrecy. In this way, lashing back or giving in undermine parental presence and increase the level of risk. Many parents do both, giving in and lashing back alternately. The resulting damage is the product of those two errors.

Determined and persistent vigilant care can reduce both the conflict and the danger. A parent who feels sure that her acts are necessary for the child's safety will avoid unnecessary clashes and radiate a sense of determination. Abiding by one's duty without a show of indignation, a threatening display or an attempt at retaliation increases the chances that the child will gradually adapt.

From time to time, most parents need to refresh their ability to withstand their child's invitations to escalate. To help them do this, we formulated the following points that serve as a kind of parental meditation, a mantra of vigilant care and self-control:

> "Exercising vigilant care is a major parental duty. If I neglect it, I hurt my child. When warning signs appear, I have to intensify my vigilance."

> "I don't have to convince my child that my attitude is justified. I only have to tell myself: 'I cannot give up on my child!'"

> "If I let my child engage me in pointless discussions, I'll undermine my decisiveness and increase her resistance."

> "I don't have to prove to my child that I have solid evidence to intensify my vigilance. My vigilance is dictated not by proofs, but by warning signals that I detect."

> "My child may attack me so as to prevent my acts of vigilant care. In such cases I have to remind myself: 'Don't argue!' 'Don't get carried away!' 'Don't retaliate!'"

> "If I maintain my self-control when provoked, I am a strong and caring parent. If I get carried away, I cease to be an anchor for my child and instead become her ping-pong ball."

> "I cannot act alone. I must widen my base by including relatives, friends, teachers, and parents of my child's friends. Asking for help is not a sign of weakness, but rather serves to broaden my shoulders as a parent."

"Increasing my vigilance won't bring immediate results. Improvements will be gradual and often partial. But the level of danger will diminish, and I'll be more able to protect my child in case of need."

"If I make mistakes, tomorrow is a new day. I can rebuild my commitment and develop better self-control."

"If my child threatens me with dire consequences for my acts of vigilant care, I can tell her: 'I'll do all in my power to prevent you from realizing your threat, except giving up on you!'"

"If I am afraid of my child's threats, I have to prepare myself so as to prevent the dangerous acts they imply. Preparation reduces risk and conflict. Giving in brings new threats and increased dangers."

We often give parents this text at the end of a course on vigilant care. It is a kind of diploma that summarizes the main challenges in dealing with a resistant child. It helps parents take a deep breath and collect themselves in situations where previously the urgency to react sharply might have prevailed. Rehearsing the text helps the parents' voice change from a short-lived clamor into a steady presence. This is the voice of vigilant care, and when parents think, feel and act this way, it passes from the parents' hearts into the heart of the child.

Preparing to Deal with Threats

Parents need to have a plan to deal with the situations they fear. Timely preparation prevents helplessness and impulsiveness. Some parents are deterred by the thought that they should prepare in advance for extreme reactions. However, when those worries are already present in the parents' minds, the best option is to develop a coping strategy. It makes it easier for parents to do so if they understand that the very process of preparation reduces risk. The gain is double: preparation diminishes the threat and if the threat materializes, it helps parents react in ways that reduce damage.

The Support Network

The first step in preparing oneself to deal with serious threats is to assemble a support group. Parents who stand alone are much more helpless and afraid. The importance of the support network that we described in the routine practice of vigilant care grows enormously when the parents are faced with more extreme scenarios. Children's threats, like all forms of blackmail, are much more effective with an isolated recipient. In effect, children often threaten with extreme retaliation if the parents involve outsiders. If the parents comply, the immediate fear may abate somewhat, but the actual danger to which the child is exposed increases.

Basically, any person who has some significant contact with the parents, or can get in touch with the child, can help the parents cope with the threat. Support groups often include grandparents, uncles, aunts, cousins, older siblings, in-laws, the parents' friends, friends from work, neighbors, parents of the child's friends and even friends from the past. On the professional side, teachers, youth instructors, sport coaches, community police, church members or members of voluntary associations can provide valuable help. Sometimes some of the child's friends help.

The natural tendency of many parents is to reduce to a minimum the list of candidates in their support network. Our goal is to help the parents overcome this tendency, as a sizable support group allows for effective actions that would be difficult with a very small one. Parents who become used to a restricted social sphere—often because of the child's problems—may find it hard to approach other people for help, because they believe others are too busy with their own problems to be willing to help. It helps them to know that parents in similar situations, who dared to break out of their isolation, found that most of the people they approached reacted positively and in many cases were not only able to provide encouragement and moral support, but also some real practical help. Gradually, most parents are able to enlarge their support group, often beginning with a limited circle and, as they gain some experience in the process, broadening it according to need. However, when parents are confronted with a very acute threat, this can be used as a platform to recruit supporters on a wider basis. Emergencies provide legitimacy, making parents willing to act in ways that in other circumstances would be too difficult for them. We remind the parents that the child will react to the parental disclosure similarly whether the parents recruit five or ten supporters. Therefore it is advisable to take advantage of the momentum created by the emergency to broaden the support network as much as possible (Omer & Dolberger, 2015).

The best way to approach a supporter is to tell her what is happening in plain terms. For instance: "Lately, I've become more and more worried about my daughter. I'm afraid she's hiding things from me and is getting into real trouble. Can we meet and talk about that?" Or, "In the last few months, my wife and I have realized that our son has made some very dangerous friendships. He also changed his behavior toward us, is evasive and abusive, and when we ask him where he's going, he slams the door and vanishes." The parents' candid talk inspires feelings of empathy and identification. This is especially clear with other parents. Probably there is hardly a parent who, upon hearing such a request, will not say to himself: "This could happen to me, too!" Some say openly: "I'd be happy to meet with you, I have similar concerns regarding my daughter!"

In the meeting, the help-seeking parent should describe the problematic situation in detail. Parents in our program are encouraged to say: "I am in the middle of a learning process. I'm trying to improve my vigilance and look after my child more closely. I now understand that if I remain alone with the problem, I'll be much weaker. That's why I dared to take this step and ask for help." A supporter who gets detailed information will usually become more involved and effective. The more open and candid the parent, the greater the supporter's potential help.

The basic request from every supporter is that she come and visit the family. The best time for a home visit is when the child is there. If, however, the visit takes place when the child is absent, the supporter can leave him a short positive message or a symbolic gift (such as an ornament for the room, or a photo reminding the child of a joint event). The parents can ask the supporter to prepare something in advance. Such visits and symbolic gifts tend to waken the child's dormant sense of belonging. If the supporter does not know the child (for instance, one of the parents' co-workers), it is important that the parents tell the child in advance that they are going to receive visits from friends who want to help them cope with the difficult time they are having. Thus, even if the child is not at home or is not acquainted with some of the supporters, the mere visit changes something in the family atmosphere. The parents must prepare for their child's angry reaction, such as: "How dare you talk about me with strangers?" The best way to answer is to calmly state: "We feel that we're going through a difficult period and decided to get all the help we can get." Even if the child reacts sourly, the goal has been achieved: the parents have shown that they decided to break out of their isolation.

When the supporter has a personal relationship with the child, she can add: "I know that you're going through a difficult period at home. You're very important to me, and I'd be glad to help you in any way I can!" If the child prevents any direct communication (for instance, by locking himself in his room), the supporter can leave a written message. Usually the child will not respond to the message. But he knows that the supporter was there and is willing to help. He also knows that the parents asked for help. Home visits lend depth to the parents' position. Their presence is now amplified and validated.

The Threat of Running Away

Many children threaten to run away. Some act in ways that increase the parents' fears. Images of the child roaming in dangerous places or descending into drug addiction, delinquency or prostitution, haunt the parents' minds. The threat also reinforces feelings of guilt, as parents brood over how they brought the child to this point. Fear, guilt and the wish to prevent disconnection combine to paralyze them. However, parents can re-anchor themselves even in such difficult situations.

Myra's (17) scholastic performance fell drastically in the course of the last year. She only continued going to school because of her new friends, all of whom were problem students. Her parents Guy and Liza felt that Myra was becoming more and more detached from them, spending most of her time with her new friends. They tried to confront her and define clear rules about when she should be back at night, but Myra reacted by secluding herself in her room for two whole days. After that, she left home at night without notifying her parents and slept over at a friend's, whom the parents did not know. She came back the next day with a tongue piercing. When her mother tried to ask her about her disappearance and the piercing, she answered that the parents were pushing her away completely. In the following months, Myra shut herself up in her room or slept outside the house without saying where she was. Guy and Liza walked on eggshells out of fear that Myra would disappear. In their first counseling session, the parents were helped to understand that the way they were behaving conveyed to Myra a message of despair. They were helped to build a network of support, and got in touch with a couple of Myra's friends and their parents. They prepared to withstand the expected confrontation with Myra without lashing back or giving in. In the counseling sessions, they role-played those situations. When Myra vanished once more, they contacted her friends, located her and arrived at the house where she was staying. They were shown into the house and Myra was asked down to meet with them. Myra seemed totally shocked when she saw them. Guy told her calmly but firmly that they wanted to take her home. Myra did not say a word. Liza said they were there because they cared for her and would not give up on her, and she asked her again to go home with them. When her friend's mother told her that she was welcome to come back the next day, but asked her to go home with her parents, she reluctantly agreed. In the following days, a number of supporters visited the house, and two of them succeeded in talking to Myra. Gradually, Myra started to participate in the family meals. In the summer, she held a job for two months. After discussing her options with one of the supporters, she told her parents she was willing to join a special program for kids who were in danger of dropping out of school. Both Myra and her parents knew they couldn't be overly optimistic, but all three felt less despairing than before.

A child whose threats of running away prevent his parents from taking action to protect him is hurled into a void. The parents' helplessness is like a rupture of the anchor's cable, precisely at the moment when the currents are about to carry the ship away. For the child, the parents' passivity is the final proof that they are no longer there for him. In such a situation, the attraction exercised by his problematic friends will grow. If, however, the parents succeed in showing determination in their care, this may leave a hopeful sign in the child's mind, even if he does not explicitly acknowledge this.

By putting into action their plan to look for their truant child, the parents create an experience of presence. Sometimes the very hardships of the search, and the difficult situation in which they find their child, serve to reinforce the child's feeling that the parents love him and are willing to fight for him:

> Irving (17) came home under the influence of alcohol or drugs a number of times. After his parents, Arthur and Silvia, caught him stealing his mother's jewelry, he ran away from home. The parents, who had been prepared for this eventuality, got in touch with some of his friends, who told them they were in touch with him. The parents decided not to alert the police, especially as Irving's friends told them that if the police were notified, Irving would react in an extreme way. None of them was willing to give the parents any additional information. Thereupon the parents widened their search, contacted additional kids who had been Irving's friends in the past and finally succeeded in discovering where he was staying. Arthur arrived accompanied by his brother, and found Irving asleep on a mattress. The floor was a jumble of cigarette stubs, empty beer cans and bottles of vodka. Arthur woke him up from a very deep sleep. When Irving opened his eyes, he was stunned to see his father before him. He asked: "How did you find me?" Arthur answered him: "We'll always find you, because we won't stop looking for you!" Irving agreed to go home with his father. In the following days, many people visited him at home, among them some of his older friends, from the times when Irving was not involved with drugs and alcohol. Irving responded well to those visits. They talked about things they used to do together and helped Irving to start thinking about how to go back to a more normal life.

Irving's feeling of relief was probably not only due to the fact that his father had found him. The very search, the attempts to make contact and the messages he received from his friends were signs of love and devotion. A young person's experience of "being found" by his parents implies that they have been looking for him intensively. This feeling counteracts the sense of abandonment experienced by young people who feel their parents have given up on them in despair. This situation was immortalized in the episode in which Tom Sawyer vanishes from home and hides on an island in the river, from where he follows with fascination the attempts of the whole village to find him. The experience of being looked for can be very meaningful, becoming treasured in the child's heart, even if he does not acknowledge it openly.

In order to prepare themselves to cope with the threat of running away, parents should collect names and phone numbers from all the people who could be in touch with their child. People who were linked to him in the past can also prove significant. Their importance can manifest itself after the child returns, as they become part of the support network that surrounds him and his parents. Each new person on the list may bring another name and another contact. The parents' very attempt to reach out to those people reflects their readiness to stay close.

Through this preparatory work, the parents become progressively aware of the child's social reality. The assumption that the child's friends, being part of the child's problem, will not be willing to help is mistaken. This parental attitude actually perpetuates the chasm between the adult world and the world of "irresponsible" kids. In reality, the parents' willingness to contact the child's friends creates islands of parental presence in the child's surroundings. Those contact points can turn into bridgeheads for the parents' attempts to reach out to their child.

Contacting the parents of the child's friends can also be highly significant. Every parent in that group should be viewed as a potential ally. The assumption that those are problematic parents who will not cooperate is not a valid one. Even a problematic parent may respond positively if approached in a positive and respectful way. Asking those parents for a small helping act, while promising to do the same for them if the occasion arises, can at times turn an apparently incapable parent into a meaningful ally. The secret of those seemingly improbable alliances lies in our understanding that, deep in their hearts, those parents may also have warm parental feelings that were frustrated by the tragic conditions of their lives. If we address those deep-seated parental wishes, we may find them willing to help. After all, we are now in the same boat with them.

When the child is found, it is crucial to avoid any physical confrontation or attempt to force the child to return home. Such attempts often lead to frightful escalation. If the child runs away from the parents, he should not be pursued. It is much better to stay in place and use the opportunity to spark up a conversation with his friends. Such conversations may create new contacts, which, at times, can prove invaluable.

> Mario told his son Carlos (13) that he would punish him severely if he failed to abide by the curfew limitations. The father was worried that Carlos was going out nightly with a group of older friends, who were suspected of stealing motorcycles and going out on sprees. Instead of answering, Carlo went to his room and locked his door. He later left by the window and stayed out, in defiance of his father's prohibition. Mario went out to look for him and found him on a street corner in the company of his friends. Mario got out of the car, approached his son and ordered him peremptorily to get into the car. When Carlos refused, he twisted his arm and forced him into the car. Before dawn, Carlos jumped out of the window again and disappeared. Mario called the police. When the police found him, Carlos did not hesitate to tell them that his father had hit him in front of his

friends. Mario was taken into custody and legal proceedings were opened against him. From that moment on, he felt his hands were tied. He had no doubt that Carlos would not flinch from getting him into deeper trouble if he tried to cross him.

Some parents believe that any attempt of theirs to look for the truant child will only make her go farther away. The only real option in their eyes is that the child achieve an inner spontaneous change—for instance, through therapy. This is probably an illusion. When parents stop exercising vigilant care, and instead rely on individual psychotherapy to do the job, the deterioration usually continues unabated (Borduin et al., 1995). Therapy for the child can only be helpful if the parents exercise vigilant care. The worst possible solution is to agree to the child's demand, that if she is willing to go to therapy, the parents will stop calling and searching for her. Under those conditions, the child's therapy becomes an obstacle to vigilant care. If the parents ask any questions, the child answers: "I am in therapy and those are private things that I discuss with my therapist!"

The parents' assumption that searching for the child is useless, as the child can always run away again, is unjustified. If the parents are deterred by the magnitude of the task, they can place a limit on their search activities. For instance, they can decide they will perform three searches, including visits to street corners and friends' houses, pausing for one week after each search. In between, they will make telephone rounds, leaving messages for the child with all the friends they contact.[1] Such a well-defined and delimited plan may give the parents enough strength to abide by their decision. Actually, in most cases, the parents do not even have to reach the limit of street searches they set for themselves, as after a couple of such events, some positive changes become manifest. Most parents who have experimented with those activities discover that in a matter of weeks, their situation changes from one of total disconnection and lack of knowledge to one in which they feel they have valuable contact points, know more about what is going on in their child's life and have an ear to the ground.

Preparing for the child's running away may be important in itself, even if the child never realizes her threat. The preparation rescues the parents from helplessness, allowing them to exercise vigilant care in spite of the child's threats. Moreover, parental preparation reduces the risk that the child will attempt running away, because the parents now have an ear to the ground. In contrast, parents who allow the threat to paralyze them increase the risk.

Suicide Threats[2]

The fear of suicide is the worst of all parental horror scenarios. Other damages can be repaired, but suicide is an act of absolute finality. The fear of suicide lurks in the mind of many parents, even when the child has never made an explicit threat. Needless to say, the parents of a child who openly threatens suicide or makes a suicidal gesture may live in constant dread. We recommend to those parents to get help from a professional that has experience in dealing with suicidal youth. Under no circumstances should they ignore the threat or keep it secret. At the risk of laboring this point, we want to stress that individual psychotherapy for the child is only relevant when the parents continue to exercise vigilant care. If the child's threats succeed in reducing the parents to inactivity, the situation only gets worse.

In order not to hurt the child's development or aggravate suicidal risk in the long run, parents should maintain reasonable expectations of normal functioning from their child, even in the face of a suicidal threat. This is particularly true in the case of children who are in danger of dropping out of school or are in a process of social withdrawal. Many parents allow their child to stay home when they feel the child has a hard time coping with school, friends or other life challenges. When the framework that maintains the child's functioning is dismantled in the wake of threats, various negative processes ensue:

- The child's coping attempts, which constitute the main defense against anxiety and depression, cease.
- The child's social ties are reduced.
- Dropping out of school (and other social frameworks) hurts the child's self-esteem and deepens despair.

The ensuing combination of passivity, isolation and despair increases suicidal risk to levels higher than those of the initial crisis. However, when the child sees that her parents are willing to fight for her and to resist her tendency to drop out and withdraw into herself, loneliness and despair can gradually be reduced, even if the child makes a show of anger at the parents' attempts. Moreover, the parents' struggle keeps them present in the child's life, so that they are more aware of what is going on and better able to protect the child.

Parents who live in fear that their child may commit suicide imagine that the child is walking on the edge of a precipice and that any additional pressure will make her jump. Many children nurture those parental fears with signs that they may commit suicide. Parents sometimes argue over whether those signs are real or manipulative. When one of the parents believes they are manipulative, the other may become even more determined to protect the child against a hostile world that now includes the blaming parent as well. Thus, the angrier one parent is, the more protective the other becomes. In effect, the distinction between "real" and "manipulative" is irrelevant. The child's suffering at school or in the company of other kids is real enough. The child feels the need to voice her distress cogently, so as to get the parents' help in protecting her. The vital question is then not whether the child is putting on a show, but how to find ways to protect her without relinquishing basic expectations of acceptable functioning. Complying with the child's wish to be left alone will leave her in a deeply negative situation. In contrast, when the parents maintain their presence and, instead of leaving her alone, actually bring in additional support, they reduce her hopelessness and isolation.

Parents often fear that the child will refuse the help of the supporters so as to punish them for revealing her secret. In effect, some children protest harshly, sometimes boycotting the supporters. However, in the majority of cases, the child ends up accepting help, at least from one of the supporters. The child's despair is already diminished even before she accepts any actual help. Phone calls and written messages from the supporters do not leave her unaffected, even when she makes a show of indifference. Each and every offer of support signals a possible way out of her plight. The greater the distress, the more relevant the offers of help. The reason is that the precipice is not only alluring, but also deeply frightening, and as the child approaches it, her readiness to grasp at the hands that are stretched out to her grows.

The presence of a support group modifies the communication about suicide in yet another way. Suicidal threats have maximum impact when only the parents are involved. The enclosed parent–child environment constitutes ideal surroundings for the amplification of suicide threats. The suicidal tendency is not hermetically enclosed within the child's mind, but is fed by continuous interaction with the parents. As this problematic communication becomes established, the suicidal thoughts in the child's mind may be strengthened. This "suicidal ecology" is changed completely once the environment includes not only the parents, but also other supporters. In the presence of supporters, suicide signals are no longer nurtured, but gradually recede, while other forms of communication take their place. Suicide ideation is not independent of suicidal communication: when the communication is altered and new forms of exchange appear, the child's mind becomes less dominated by thoughts of suicide. Therefore, we suggest that each and every time the child alludes to the possibility of suicide, parents should call at least one of the supporters. The parent must not do this demonstratively, calling the supporter in the child's presence. It is better to do this discreetly, asking the supporter to visit or contact the child by phone. This kind of response releases the parents from their automatic response to the child's invitation to a new bout of suicidal interaction.

> Bob (18) became depressed when he performed poorly an athletic competition for which he had prepared for over a year. He threw away the expensive shoes that his parents had bought him for the occasion and declared he was giving up all sports activities. The crisis deepened when Bob found out that because he had invested so much effort in sports, he had failed three important exams. He blamed his parents for having been blind to his situation. The accusations gradually grew and Bob started blaming his parents for all the mistakes he believed that they had committed in the past.

He made innuendos that suggested he didn't care to go on living. The innuendos developed into open threats that were accompanied by veritable orgies of blame. Twice, he entered their room in the middle of the night, screaming horribly and throwing objects against the walls. The parents' worries grew when Bob started to leave home for long hours during the night. They made an appointment with a psychiatrist, but Bob refused to come. They came to our center for consultation and, with the therapist's help, they built a support group made up of relatives, friends, Bob's sport coach and two of Bob's best friends. A temporary calm was achieved when Bob's uncle invited him to stay with him for a few weeks. Bob agreed, and at first seemed to be pulling himself together. However, when the mother visited, Bob renewed his threats, locked himself in the bathroom and refused to answer when she or the uncle tried to talk with him from behind the door. He then left the house without saying where he was going. It seemed that when the parents were around, the threats resurfaced. This led to the decision that, in the upcoming weeks, all communication with Bob would be maintained by the supporters. In the beginning, Bob was very angry that his secret had been exposed. He told the supporters who called him that they could not help him. However, he agreed to allow a few of them to visit him. In the three days that followed the clash with his mother, five supporters visited him at his uncle's. On the third night, as Bob seemed to be especially restless, his uncle and his sports coach succeeded in convincing him to go out with them for a long walk. They stayed with him through the night. The companionship that he felt in this long night created a special bond between Bob, his uncle and the sports coach. In the following days, the exchanges with his uncle and the sports coach were conducted in more positive tones. Bob's emotional situation remained difficult for a while, but the suicidal messages ended. Direct contact with the parents was renewed a month later, after Bob agreed to take part in a community program involving school help, sports and social activities.

The parents of children with less difficult conditions may wonder whether such an extreme example can be of relevance to them. In effect, many parents worry about suicide, even though the child does not display extreme behaviors. In such cases, developing a coping scenario can help the parents reduce both the anxiety and the actual risk. Moreover, if the child does voice threats, the parents can respond in a way that will prevent common errors, such as keeping the problem secret or ceasing all demands and expectations of normal functioning. With the help of a coping scenario, parents will know that they must not remain alone with the problem or free the child from all demands and expectations. Involving supporters when the child begins expressing threats or innuendos rapidly changes the suicidal ecology, often leading to a quick reduction in the level of risk.

Notes

1 A detailed parents' manual for telephone rounds and street visitations appears in Omer (2004).
2 We have dealt with this matter in detail in Omer, H. & Dolberger, D. (2015).

References

Borduin, C. M., Cone, L. T., Barton, J. M., Henggeler, S. W., Rucci, B. R., Blaske, D. M. & Williams, R. A. (1995). Multi-systemic treatment of serious juvenile offenders: Long-term prevention of criminality and violence. *Journal of Consulting and Clinical Psychology*, *63*: 569–578.

Gilligan, S. (1987). Therapeutic trances: The cooperation principle in Ericksonian hypnotherapy. New York: Brunner/Mazel [Routledge].

Omer, H. (2004). *Non-Violent Resistance: A new approach to violent and self-destructive children*. New York and Cambridge: Cambridge University Press.

Omer, H. & Dolberger, D. I. (2015). Helping parents cope with suicide threats: An approach based on non-violent resistance. *Family Process*, *10*: 1–17.

Padilla-Walker, L. M., Nelson, L. J. & Knapp, D. J. (2014). "Because I'm still the parent, that's why!" Parental legitimate authority during emerging adulthood. *Journal of Social and Personal Relationships*, *31*(3): 293–313.

Patterson, G. R., Dishion, T. J. & Bank, L. (1984). Family interaction: A process model of deviancy training. *Aggressive Behavior*, *10*: 253–267.

4   Lies

with Shai Satran

Parents often find themselves in dilemmas regarding lies. Sometimes they feel that lying should be strictly forbidden; sometimes that they should regard their child's lies facetiously or even actively enable them. This often leads to confusion, particularly with children who tend to use lies to further their ends. In this chapter, we will try to understand why parents often react to the child's lies in ways that aggravate the problem and damage the parent–child relationship. We will then propose a vigilant care approach that may help parents deal with this thorny problem.

The discovery that lying is possible is part of normal development. Children develop the understanding that one's thoughts and those of others are not totally transparent at an early age (Evans & Lee, 2013). This discovery opens up the possibility of lying. At the same time, it is an important step in the development of *mentalization*—that is, the ability to see human acts as expressions of mental processes, such as thoughts, intentions and feelings (Fonagy, Gyorgy, Jurist & Target, 2004). Thus, the same cognitive achievement that enables lying allows for the development of an interpersonal skill (mentalization) that is crucial for interpersonal functioning. By and by, children also learn that they should not share everything with others, or at least not in every situation. Every child must learn this, in order to become a functioning member of society. The flip side of these abilities is, of course, lying (Lee, 2013).

Many parents are shocked when they catch their child lying: "Where did she learn that? We don't lie at home!" The answer is simple: The child learned it by herself. The question then is whether the child will become accustomed to lying in order to obtain her goals. This depends on her interaction with her surroundings. Most children will experiment with lying in some way or another. Some lie just for the pleasure of exercising a new skill. They play mental hide and seek, hiding behind the curtain of their consciousness. These children are like the Chinese, who discovered gunpowder ahead of the Europeans, but did not use it for warfare. However, some children try to use their new skill to further their goals at a very young age. The parents' role is to prevent such habits from taking root, as they can harm the moral and social development of their child. But we must remember that the ability to lie cannot be eliminated.

School-aged children can already rate lies according to their gravity. Thus, lying with the goal of avoiding punishment is perceived as worse than a lie that is meant to shield a friend from punishment. Lies that afford privileges at the expense of others are rated as even worse. And lies intended to harm others are rated as the worst (Bussey, 1999; Peterson, Peterson & Seto, 1983). These ratings are consistent, and demonstrate that children's judgment of lies is based on moral principles and not merely according to their degree of deviation from truth. Therefore, relating to the goals and consequences of the child's lies allows parents to assume a more productive stance than engaging in the futile task of trying to eradicate each and every lie. Thus, different lies require different reactions. Playful lies will be met with a playful reaction (a wink or a joke), while serious lies deserve reactions of a different kind.

Developmental Consequences of Lying

Lies can harm normal development in several ways: They can perpetuate situations in which the child doesn't fulfill his tasks; hurt the child's relationships with others; and increase exposure to temptations and dangerous influences (Warr, 2007). Lies can have cumulative effects—for instance, lying about one's homework can entail scholastic failure, which in turn may impact on the child's choice of friends, which can entail problematic activities requiring further lying, and so forth.

> Ruth (8) stopped doing her homework, even though she could have done it without difficulty. At first, it was just an exercise here and there; then there were whole pages of omitted assignments, and gradually she found herself months behind on her schoolwork. The more she fell behind, the more she worried she would be found out. When asked by her mother whether she had homework, she would deny it vigorously. This eventually aroused her mother's suspicion. After a few pointed questions and a phone call to the teacher, the scope of the deception became clear. Ruth's mother demanded that she complete all the missed tasks, and allotted a set time every day for that task. A month later, she had caught up. The mother's discovery of Ruth's deceit resulted in intensifying her vigilant care. Two years later, Ruth told her mother that being found out and helped to close the gap had brought her deep relief.

Lies regarding schoolwork and behavior can expand in worrisome ways. In adolescence, habitual lying may increase the child's risk of dropping out of school, a situation that is strongly associated with delinquency (Loeber, 1990; Warr, 2007). In those cases, lying is often accompanied by other problematic behaviors that go against social norms and expectations. Gradually, concealment becomes a lifestyle, whereby the dangerous aspects of the child's life continue to develop out of sight of the parents.

> Clara (14) began skipping school by hiding in the vicinity of home until her mother (Sylvia), a hardworking divorcée, left for work. When she saw her mother drive away, she would return home and spend the morning watching television. At first she did this occasionally, but gradually she began spending more and more days at home. The situation remained undiscovered for quite a while, because earlier in the year Sylvia had had a falling out with Clara's homeroom teacher and there was no communication between the two. Months passed until the mother realized the gravity of the problem. In addition, Sylvia discovered that Clara had been using her credit card without her knowledge. She had begun by ordering pizza, then apps and games, and then clothing. The mother brought Clara to a psychologist, but Clara stopped after one session, screaming at Silvia that she was the one who needed a shrink.

In this example, we see the gradual deterioration of the mother–daughter bond. According to the mother, they had a good and open relationship until middle school, but since that time middle school worse and worse. We can assume that Clara's lies had their roots in earlier difficulties with her mother, but they probably played a role in aggravating those problems. Lies create rifts in any close relationship. Parents of children who lie to them on a regular basis have repeated experiences of anger and estrangement. They occasionally try to convince the child to stop lying, but those attempts often become mechanical exhortations or mere threatening gestures. From the child's perspective, she feels more and more under attack and has no choice but to harden her protective shell.

At times, the web of lies creates an entire underground world, in which the child is no longer accessible to the influence of parents or other responsible adults. Instead, she aligns herself with a group of peers with whom she feels a sense of belonging and loyalty. Often, lying to parents and other grown-ups is a basic condition of group belonging. Demonstrating the readiness and capacity to conceal and lie, especially in regard to the group's disruptive activities, is then part of the initiation ceremony that gains right of entrance to the inner circle of friends.

The Attempt to Prove to the Child That He Is Lying

Though lying, as we saw, is a complex behavior, the child should hear the parents say: "Don't lie!" "That's not true!" and "I'm angry at you because of your lie!" A parent who does not label lying negatively causes moral confusion. In time, children become able to differentiate between "real lies" and "playful lies," as well as to know which lies are totally unacceptable. But to achieve this, they have to begin with a clear and simple concept about lying and its undesirability.

However, even when they make their position clear, parents often find that their child continues lying in unacceptable ways. Lying may then become an habitual tool that the child uses to get out of unpleasant situations. When the parents catch their child lying, they often try to prove it to the child in the hope that he will admit it and stop lying. To their amazement, they often find that the child reacts by entrenching himself even further in his lies. Why does this happen?

Children who habitually lie often feel overburdened by demands and expectations. For these children, lying is an umbrella that protects them from the experience of constantly not living up to expectations. The parents' explanations, lectures, accusations and threats fall upon them like a steady downpour. In order to protect themselves, they learn to treat the parents' exhortations as so much background noise. The parents' threats and screams are then just the usual thunder that accompanies the storm.

When faced with the child's lies, the parents feel obliged to check what is really happening. However, there is a deep difference between an inspection based on parental vigilant care and the collection of evidence to prove to the child that he is lying. In the latter case, the parents expect the child to bow his head in surrender. This expectation is not only futile, but also deeply harmful. Each new round of accusation and denial increases the damage. The parent–child relationship turns into a court of law, in which the parents' purpose is to obtain and present damning evidence, while the child becomes adept at tergiversation and postponement. The worst moment is probably when the child is confronted with "the crushing evidence" that proves him guilty beyond a shadow of a doubt. In presenting their evidence, the parents actually preclude all possibility of cooperation because the child perceives bowing his head in such a situation as a deep humiliation. No wonder most children in this situation refuse to surrender. Some do this by a show of defiance. Others cloak themselves in impenetrable silence. Many nurture a deep wish for revenge.

Intensifying Vigilant Care

The restoration of full parental trust after repeated lying would mean a decrease in vigilant care when the child most needs it, leaving him to face temptation and social pressure on his own. Ironically, what appears to be a loving act of full trust turns out to be more an act of abandonment. In contrast, the limited trust of vigilant care, which grows when the child cooperates but diminishes when he is evasive, confers an experience of parental presence and offers the child an anchor to help him regain his stability.

The positive alternative of intensifying vigilant care is based on the understanding that lying cannot be totally eradicated and that the child cannot be forced into submission. A child who lies needs parents who are closer and more present, rather than effective prosecutors.

The parents can, for instance, tell the child: "When you are evasive, I check more. When you're open and reliable, I give you more credit." This message makes it clear that trust is a matter of degree. The all-or-nothing dichotomy of *trust or no trust* makes life impossible. When parents and child think in these absolute terms, even a perfectly justified inquiry on the parents' part can lead to the accusation "You don't trust me!" This makes the parents feel guilty and think they are being unfair and failing their child in providing an experience of trust. However, every parent knows that trust can shrink or expand according to the child's behavior. This understanding serves as an antidote to the child's angry accusation. The honest answer on the parents' side would be, "It's true that my trust has been shaken. But I'd like to trust you more, and will do so as things get better." This message is especially helpful when it is backed by a supporter, who can say to the child: "I talked to your mother, and she really wants to be able to trust you more. You can help in that, and I'm ready to help you help her!"

Vigilant care also means that the parents have a right to doubt. The parents can say: "Because of what happened in the last few weeks, I've really begun to doubt what you say. So I'll keep my eyes open!" In this way, parents candidly express their doubt, without explicitly telling the child that they believe he is lying. Such an accusation, particularly if made in a belligerent tone, would inevitably lead to escalation. In contrast, when the parents manifest their doubt in a matter-of-fact way, they can prevent escalation, while underscoring that trust and vigilance regulate each other.

This approach also allows parents to avoid positioning themselves as judges in conflicts between siblings. Instead of trying to answer impossible questions, like the eternal "Who started it?" the parents can say: "At the moment I am not sure of anything, but I will keep an eye on what is happening!" To do this, the parents must understand that they cannot come up with an answer to the children's contradictory versions. In all probability, any "guilty verdict" on their part would lead to a feeling of betrayal by one of the children (and often by both, especially as the supposedly guilty party often refuses to abide by the parents' verdict). If, however, the parents avoid ruling on "what happened," and instead choose to intensify their vigilance, they diminish the experience of abandonment.

Nathan (9) ran to his mother in tears, claiming that his twin brother Jerry had hit him. Jerry is stronger than Nathan, and there had been frequent fights in the last few months. While Nathan is weaker, he is sly and his mother knew that he often tended to distort and exaggerate. Later in the evening, the parents sat with Jerry and Nathan, and told them that they were going to watch over them closely. They said that hitting would be punished, but that they would not act upon reports, but look for themselves. They were backed by the grandparents, who told the siblings the next day that they supported the parents and would uphold their decision when the children were at their house. When Jerry protested that this was not fair because Nathan lied, the grandfather answered: "Then it's good for you that we'll be watching closely. We'll then see that you are controlling yourself and not hitting him. It will prove you are blameless!" To Nathan, the grandfather said: "You'll be more protected, because we'll be watching you both more closely!" The parents then made sure the door to the boys' room always remained open. One of the parents would sometimes come in and stand for a minute in the room. The hitting incidents and complaints diminished. The siblings also became better able to sort things out between themselves, without recourse to lies or violence.

Diminishing parental involvement when signs of danger recede is important to the development of self-care. Parents must allow a growing child more space when the demands of safety are reasonably fulfilled. Donald Winnicott's classical *good enough mother* should be attentive and attuned, but not overly so. Otherwise, the child would not grow. Thus, it is good that the mother has her moments of fatigue, as well as other duties and roles, because without that the child would not have the opportunity to learn how to regulate her emotions and care for herself. Vigilant care is similar. Children need parents to be *vigilant enough*, but it is their limitations that enable the child to develop self-care. When the parent says to the child: "The more you keep me in the loop, the less I interfere," she is conveying a message to the child and to herself. She is reminding herself that her parenting task is limited. One must keep a finger on the pulse, but also maintain an honest willingness to let go.

Interpersonal and Disciplinary Consequences of Lying

It may be disappointing to realize that the wish to completely root out lying is unrealistic, as lying has its roots in normal cognitive development. However, relinquishing the wish for total control does not mean that lying is devoid of interpersonal and disciplinary consequences.

Parents are often amazed when we recommend that they tell their child, "Our trust in you has been shaken." And yet, this is the most important message in cases of lying or concealment. The understanding that trust is a delicate aspect of any relationship, and that once it is broken it cannot be fully restored, is central to the child's development. The fall from grace that results from the loss of absolute trust is not easy, but the clock cannot be turned back. A child who uses lying to achieve his own goals ends his age of innocence, and begins his long journey into the complexities of human relations. Total trust is a luxury that most of us cannot always afford. Actually, it is the awareness that trust is not absolute that is often vital for the maintenance of a healthy relationship.

Trusting less and checking more are not punishments in the traditional sense, but rather natural consequences of lying. A parent who tries to protect the child from this natural consequence leaves him exposed to negative developments. A loving parent will always give his child another chance, but the past must not be erased, on pain of compromising the future. The child needs to understand that rebuilding trust is a gradual process. Every effort in this direction should be acknowledged, and every sign of trustworthiness applauded, so that in time both sides may enjoy more trust. This hard-earned trust is an achievement, surely more so than pristine trust, but they are definitely not the same.

Violations of trust have consequences that go beyond the parent–child relationship. They also entail a narrowing of the child's autonomous space. Parents now demand that the child report more, and they supervise more closely. They can also make it clear that it is the intensification of their vigilance that, in time, may allow for their trust to grow again. The "punishment" thus opens the way for its own cancellation.

> Sheila (16) said angrily that there was no point in trying, because her parents would not trust her in any case. A year before, after having long misled her parents about her whereabouts, school absences and test results, her parents intensified their supervision. They maintained close contact with her homeroom teacher, and made a rule that Sheila could not use the computer or the smartphone on days when she missed school or private lessons. Gradually, Sheila's scholastic functioning improved and her lying diminished. But, a year later, things got worse again. She accused her parents of not believing her anyway, so why bother? She was upset and morose, and began spending long hours in bed. The fear she was sinking into depression made her parents rethink their restrictions. However, before they turned their plan into action, they consulted with our center. The counselor thought that reversing the restrictions might actually cause more harm than good. He proposed another course of action, which the parents accepted. They began by telling Sheila: "We know that you are going through a difficult period, and we want to be there for you. Regarding our trust, you are right, it has been shaken. But we want to trust you more. We would be glad to do so if you would help us

a little. Last year, you made substantial efforts and gradually we started to trust you more. We think this can happen again!" The next day, Sheila's aunt came to her and told her: "I know your parents want to be able to trust you more. If you help, I'll help too! Trust grows step by step, and I think your efforts will pay off!" Sheila's teacher, who was also involved, told her: "You seem hopeless lately. You might be feeling that we are demanding too much from you. Let's sit down and make a plan that you feel you can cope with. I will talk to your parents, and I am sure they will accept it!" Two weeks later, there were signs of cooperation. Her aunt told her: "Your parents told me they feel things are getting better. They still check on you, but they're beginning to trust you more." Her mother said to her: "What happened last week means a lot to me!" Her father said, "Even if there are hard moments ahead, we won't forget the positive steps you've taken!" A month later, it seemed that Sheila was back to where she was before the crisis.

Children often demand that their parents keep their lies secret from the outside world, or even from the other parent. Parents should not accede to this demand. Agreeing to hide a child's lies means cooperating with the deceit and abetting its consequences. We recommend instead that the parents' acts of vigilant care be made known to the relevant people in the child's surroundings. Thus, we encourage parents to talk to the child's teacher when she lies about school issues, or check with her friends' parents when she lies about her whereabouts. Creating transparency is crucial for reducing lying.

Sean (8) used to overreact to any uncomfortable situation. His father, Eric, a school principal, was a warm person, who expressed his affection physically to his three sons. The boys enjoyed Eric's playfulness, but Sean would occasionally stop the physical play with his father, claiming he had been hurt and walking around with his arm in an unnatural position so as to accentuate the supposed injury he had suffered. Gradually, this tendency became more and more pronounced. He told people at school that his parents would leave him home alone at night in order to teach him courage. This was reported to the school counselor, who invited Sean to her office. Sean told her that his father twisted his arm, locked him in a closet and denied him food, when he did not act as expected. The school counselor reported this to the police, and Eric was arrested the very same day. Judicial proceedings were opened, and he had to leave his job as principal. Sean was sent to a therapist who also specialized in examinations for forensic purposes. In the course of the evaluation, Sean's tendency to make up stories became manifest. He told the therapist that his father used to train him for the possibility that he would be captured by the enemy and would have to withstand torture. He described how his father would take him to the desert, make him carry heavy loads, limit his drinking water, and train him how to withstand different tortures. The therapist, who had begun to suspect that Sean was fabricating, asked him if his father had ever used the torture technique in which the prisoner is tied up for hours with a water drip on his head, so as to make him think he's losing his mind. Sean said that his father had, indeed, trained him several times in that technique, until he had become able to withstand it. Gradually, it became clear that Sean was not in the least afraid of his father, but, on the contrary, claimed his father was his best friend and that their joint outings were absolute fun for both of them. In contrast to what he had told the school counselor, Sean said that his father never punished him, but only put him through courage training. After a couple of months, the charges against Eric were dismissed and the parents came to our center for help. With the therapist's help, they built a support group of relatives and close friends. Everyone in the group was aware of Sean's tendencies, and had witnessed his exaggerations and fabrications in the past. The therapist asked the parents to report to the group whenever Sean came up with new fabrications. Each time this happened, Sean would receive two phone calls from group members, saying: "I heard that you said such and such. You know, Sean, that I love you very much and think you are great, but these stories are giving you a bad reputation. People are saying you are a liar. We have to find a way to fix that!" After a week, Sean began showing signs of self-control. He would start to tell a fib, but would stop mid-sentence, adding, "No, I actually didn't want to say anything!" The therapist visited the school, and spoke with the school counselor and the homeroom teacher about the work he was doing with the family. He asked them to be in touch with him, and let him know if there was any event that required special attention. Sean's fabrications gradually disappeared. However, Sean's father felt that the damage to his name would make it impossible for him to return to his job as school principal. He decided to join his parents' family business. Only after the judicial procedure was closed was Sean told that his father had been reported to the police because of Sean's stories about tortures, but that all charges had been dropped because Sean had decided to stop telling fibs. Sean was told that though he had made a mistake, his efforts to learn to exercise self-control had helped the whole family.

When a child's lies hurt other people, the child should be helped to make amends. For instance, the parents can tell their child: "You skipped your private lesson today, telling the teacher that you were ill. But then you went to play football with your friends. We had to pay for your lesson anyhow. Now you have to find a way to make amends to us!" Any constructive proposal by the child, even if symbolic, should be accepted. However, if the child refuses, he should be told: "Think about this for three days. If you come up with your own idea it will be best. If not, we'll decide what the compensation should be." During this interval, a relative or family friend who has a good relationship with the child should tell him he is aware of the situation, and is willing to help him reach an agreement with his parents. If the child remains adamant, the supporter may tell him: "That is too bad. If your parents have to decide on the compensation by themselves, it will be much more expensive. And in that case, I'd agree with them!" Parents sometimes wonder how they can demand compensation from a child who has no money of his own. A possible way is to reduce the child's allowance. If the child does not get a regular allowance, the parents can reduce the amount of money the child is given for entertainment (for instance, paying for movie tickets, but not for popcorn, throughout one month). The supporters can also offer to help the child get a fair deal, or propose other solutions (like washing the family car). Keep in mind that the child's willingness to make amends is more important than the monetary value of the compensation.

In conclusion, the discovery of lying is part of the child's natural development. However, the child may turn this into a habit intended to avoid demands or achieve benefits. The parental response should then consist of intensifying vigilant care, involving the surroundings and creating transparency. Parents should call things by their names, talking openly about lies and the damage done to their trust. They should also talk about the harm caused to others, and demand that compensation be made. The child gradually learns that attempts at concealment may result in enhanced exposure, and that efforts to make deals with a parent to keep the truth from the other will fail. The child will surely feel uncomfortable in this process, but his gains will be considerable, as his world becomes more coherent and continuous, instead of being fragmented by walls of deceit. The relief that children who have been saved from a web of their own lies often experience and express gives us a good idea of the heavy burden that the lies had placed upon them.

References

Bussey, K. (1999). Children's categorization and evaluation of different types of lies and truths. *Child Development*, 70, 1338–1347.

Evans, A. D., & Lee, K. (2013). Emergence of lying in very young children. *Developmental Psychology*, 49, 1958–1963.

Fonagy, P., Gyorgy, G., Jurist, E. L. & Target, M. (2004). *Affect Regulation, Mentalization and the Development of the Self*. London: Karnac.

Lee, K. (2013). Little liars: Development of verbal deception in children. *Child Development Perspectives*, *7*, 91–96.
Loeber, R. (1990). Developmental and risk factors of juvenile antisocial behavior and delinquency. *Clinical Psychology Review*, *10*, 1–41.
Peterson, C. C., Peterson, J. L. & and Seeto, D. (1983). Developmental changes in ideas about lying. *Child Development*, *54*, 1529–1535.
Warr, M. (2007). The tangled web: Delinquency, deception, and parental attachment. *Journal of Youth and Adolescence*, *36*, 607–622.

5   Friends

with Gabriela Hanga

Children today are typically exposed to two major kinds of risk:

- Temptations in the outside world, like drugs, alcohol, unsafe sex and delinquency.
- The risk of seclusion in the virtual world.

Different kinds of children are usually drawn to each of those two realms. Children who are prone to risks in the outside world are typically those whose thirst for powerful stimuli is stronger than their fears, while those who are prone to seclusion are those whose anxiety proves stronger than their social needs. The first may be drawn further and further from home; the second are absorbed by the computer. Vigilant care can reduce both risks.

One of the difficulties experienced by parents of children in the first category lies in the fact that their behavior represents the normal developmental process by which children expand their autonomous space as they grow. The influence of peers increases during childhood, reaching its peak in adolescence (Brown, Bakken, Ameringer & Mahon, 2008). Paradoxically, parents who do not acknowledge this trend will usually have difficulty exercising vigilant care, as the child will experience their attempt to set limits as countering their growth. Indeed, parents inclined to anxious supervision can reduce the child's autonomous space in damaging ways (Segrin, Givertz, Swaitkowski & Montgomery, 2013). This was immortalized in the Yiddish song "On the Road Stands a Tree," which tells of a child who wants to fly up to a lonely tree that the birds had abandoned in their winter flight. The mother (Jewish of course) asks her child to put on a sweater, and then a scarf, and a coat, and gloves, and galoshes. The obedient child agrees to all her demands, but, in the end, finds himself too heavy to fly.

Jeff was a very protective father, tendencies which were further enhanced after his wife passed away. His daughter Eva (12) had always been very sensitive to her social status. Already in kindergarten, she would overreact whenever she felt the slightest snub. However, this did not prevent her from being "class queen." In elementary school, she continued enjoying high social status, or as she soon learned to say, she was "in" ("in" was the most important word in her vocabulary). When her mother passed away, Eva lost her social interests temporarily. However, when she tried to return to her usual place in the group, she discovered that her status was not as it used to be. Other girls were now "in" and, despite the loyalty of her two best friends, Eva gradually began to feel marginalized. Jeff was very involved in her life and was aware of everything that was happening to her. Every day he would ask her about her experiences at school, and she would tell him in great detail about what happened, who spoke with whom, and how she was shunned or rebuffed. Jeff asked the teacher to intervene, but nothing changed. Jeff tried to compensate by inviting Eva's friends over to their house and coming up with special events and activities so as to help her become "in" again. But the harder Jeff tried, the more Eva was disappointed. She thought only a miracle could make her as popular as she once was. As long as this did not happen, she preferred to stay by herself. Gradually, she replaced her actual social life with intense Facebook activity, often until very late at night. At times, she was unable to wake up for school. Jeff tried to cheer her up, telling her that she was loved and was potentially much more "in" than she thought. However, Jeff did not believe his own pep talks, and neither did Eva. Their conversations turned into a fixed scenario, in which Jeff took the optimistic part and she the pessimistic part. The counselor Jeff had approached told him about helicopter parents and how their protective hovering could prevent a child from becoming active and autonomous. Jeff, who already felt this was probably the case, decided to reduce his involvement. He told Eva: "I have decided that our daily talks about your social difficulties are not suitable for someone your age. From now on, I won't question you anymore, and won't expect reports from you." Surprisingly, Eva adjusted to the new rule and did not try to talk to her father about her daily disappointments. Jeff also decided that the computer would be turned off at ten o'clock at night. He told Eva that if she missed school, she would not be allowed to use the computer or smartphone for 24 hours. He also told her that the word "in" was no longer "in." He said they had been hypnotized by that word, and that it was time to break the trance. He also stopped arranging social meetings for Eva. After a while, Eva started meeting with friends, preferring to go to their places rather than inviting them over.

As the child grows, she tends less and less to imitate her parents and take them as her unique reference group, focusing more and more on the peer group (Dishion, Piehler & Myers, 2008). This process is already manifest at a very young age:

> Michael traveled with his son, Gaby (4), to visit his twin cousins, Yoram and Eliash, both Gaby's age. The three quickly formed a strong bond. One day, they managed to scare their parents: while returning from a walk in the neighborhood, they decided to disappear into a hiding place within the house. When the parents arrived home a few minutes after them, they could not find them. They started searching for them, not knowing if they were inside or outside. The children then burst from their hiding place, screaming cheerfully. The parents understood that the three had formed a very strong coalition. Their need for fellowship was manifest in the endlessly repeated expression "the same as": "I want the same as Gaby!" "I want the same as Yoram!" "I want the same as Eliash!" On returning home, Michael said he was so sick of that expression that he wanted it out of the family lexicon for at least a year.

During adolescence, the attraction to the peer group may clash with the values of the family, sometimes posing a real threat to the child or the parent–child relationship. Parents, however, must keep in mind that if they completely reject the child's new reference group, they may lose their own legitimacy in his eyes, since adolescents tend to view their friends as a major source of values and direction.

> David (14) suddenly stopped meeting with his former friends when he became close to Philip, who was four years older than him. He began returning home later at night and evaded his parents' questions regarding his activities. Although he still did well at school, his parents were worried about this friendship, feeling it was influencing David to do things that were inappropriate for his age. Therefore, they notified David they would not allow this relationship to continue, and threatened that if he disobeyed them, they would hire a detective to follow Philip. David worried this would hurt Philip, because he knew that Philip smoked pot, even though he had never done it in his presence. Despite the pain of the separation, David gave in. However, his mood dropped, he became withdrawn and neglected his schoolwork. His parents were worried, and decided to involve a friend who had a good relationship with David. David explained to this family friend that Philip was an intellectual and a highly creative person. The friend asked David if he would agree to his father meeting Philip. David agreed immediately.

> The father was willing to meet Phillip with an open mind. He found out that Philip was a person with very impressive talents (despite his young age, he already earned his living working as a translator in three different languages). The father explained his concerns to Philip, and asked whether he could call him from time to time. He said that David would be fully aware of these calls. He also clarified the boundaries regarding David's outings at night and voiced concerns about his exposure to potentially dangerous activities. Following the meeting, David renewed his relationship with Philip, but kept the time limits and accepted his father's involvement.

Vigilant care in the social domain takes place at the three levels described in the first chapter. At the level of *open attention*, the parents' goal is to manifest an open interest in the child's social activities. They ask themselves: "Do I know who my child's friends are?" "Do I know what their leisure activities are?" "Do I know their areas of interest?" They try to answer those questions by being close to the child, talking openly with him and trying to get acquainted with his friends in non-invasive ways. At the level of *focused attention*, the parents' goal is to clearly define their boundaries and the kind of information they request. They may tell the child: "I'll ask you with whom you're going out, where you're going to be, what you'll be doing and when you're coming back. So long as your answers are satisfactory, I won't disturb you!" At the level of *unilateral action*, they take actual steps to ensure the child's safety, e.g., making phone calls to the child's friends and their parents; coming to the house of friends when the child is there without permission; arriving in person on street corners or other places where the child is exposed to risk; and, if necessary, displaying tenacious but rigorously non-violent resistance to dangerous relationships (Omer, 2004).

Who Are My Child's Friends?

Many parents feel this question is not legitimate, and view the wish to know their child's friends as an invasion of her privacy. This attitude is a typical manifestation of the privacy reflex. The parents' wish to get to know their child's friends is not only legitimate, but an essential element of vigilant care. Even when there are no warning signs that indicate the child may be in trouble, the parents should show interest in her friends. If the child resents this, they should tell her candidly: "I decided it is important that I get to know your friends. I don't want to interfere, but it's my duty to know who they are!" At the level of open attention, this means knowing their names, where they got acquainted and what they like to do together. One good way to get to know them better is to invite them to stay over for dinner. This allows the parents to get a better impression of them. Additionally, a child who has dined at their table will be more accessible than one who has never done so.

The basic rules of hospitality make it acceptable and legitimate that the parents address the friend during a visit. If their child resents this, the parents may say "Whoever comes to our house is my guest! I won't be anonymous to my guests!" This basic human rule allows parents to introduce themselves to every child visiting their home. They can ask for the child's name and engage in a short exchange ("Are you a friend from school?" "Do you live nearby?"). These questions manifest the parents' right to be interested. Actually, asserting this right is more important than getting any specific information, for it puts the parents in a position to contact the friend more easily in case of need ("You remember me? I'm Jenny's mother!").

Nevertheless, parents who adhere to the privacy reflex might object: "But he's my child's guest, not mine!" This position significantly limits the parent's ability to exercise vigilant care and serve as an anchor to the child. The parental anchor must be attached to the ground in order to function. The home is the central place in which the parents cast their anchor. It is therefore imperative that parents may say and feel: "This is my house!" This attitude entitles them to decide what activities are allowed in the house. In contrast, parents who lose this feeling may find they are no longer able to prevent their child from turning his room into a drug den or a place where nightly celebrations are held behind locked doors.

Parents who are well rooted in the feeling "this is my house!" can cope with any attempts by the child to prevent them from establishing contact with his friends. An adolescent, for instance, may smuggle his friends into his room so as to avoid all contact between them and his parents. Even then, however, the rules of hospitality still apply. The mother, for instance, can knock at the door, especially if she comes protected with the right "shield," i.e., a plate of snacks and refreshments. Such an encounter allows her to introduce herself and ask the guests to introduce themselves. The mother's hospitality makes it unlikely that the friends will cooperate with the child's attempt to drive her away.

If the child is involved with a bad crowd, whom he strictly hides from his parents, it is even more important to get in touch with them. When adolescents are connected to criminal elements or are part of a gang, the danger justifies extraordinary measures. In those cases (and only then), we think it legitimate for the parents to obtain the phone numbers of the child's friends through their son's or daughter's cell phone or by asking the phone company for a record of incoming and outgoing calls. When the child fails to return home at night, or returns home drugged, or when the parents discover he has money or belongings that are unaccounted for, they should call all the numbers on the record, introduce themselves, say they are concerned for their child and ask those people who they are. If the parents' appeal is made in a respectful way, some of the respondents will likely be willing to assist. Even respondents who are wholly uncooperative do not remain indifferent and might choose to stop involving the child in their shady business. A child who is "contaminated" by parental presence is not an ideal adjunct to unlawful practices. Parents who dare to act in this way will no longer be in the dark. Sometimes they even find out that someone in the problematic circle is willing to help.

When parents discover their child is involved with bad friends, their first choice is usually to try and completely disconnect the child from them. Unfortunately, this objective is often unattainable and children maintain their problematic relationships, defiantly or clandestinely. When parents try to enforce their prohibition, the relationship with the child deteriorates. This leads to deeper helplessness and also widens the parent–child chasm.

The parents' disappointment has to do with the illusion of control. The attempt to achieve control in an area where they do not really have it may cause considerable damage. In contrast, parents who understand they have no control over the child are better able to act in ways that reduce risk. Their message is: "We have no control over you, but we have control over ourselves, and it's our utmost duty to do all we can to keep you from harm!" Instead of striving to eliminate the problematic friendships, they opt to increase their vigilant care. In this way, they no longer depend on the child's consent.

The difference between trying to control the child and controlling themselves is not merely semantic. In trying to control the child, the parents put pressure upon him (preaching, threatening and punishing). If their goal is not achieved, they often try to increase the pressure. If this also fails (as it usually does), the parent–child relationship hits rock bottom and the level of risk grows. In contrast, when they focus on doing their duty, rather than controlling the child, they intensify their vigilant care and take active steps to resist his dangerous activities. They increase their presence, recruit supporters and get in touch with the problematic group, making it clear that they will do all in their power to keep their child safe. Those steps weave a protective net around the child.

Involving Friends and Relatives

When the child hangs out with a highly problematic group, support becomes crucial. Without help, the parents' chances of increasing the child's safety are much lower. A parent who acts alone is often pushed into a corner where his options are narrowed. Thus, if the child lies or breaks curfew, the parent feels obliged to react more and more harshly. However, after the shouting, threatening and punishing are over, the parents are left empty handed. Even if the child seems to bow his head, the problematic allegiances are either pursued in secret or resumed after a short while. In contrast, reaching out to a support group allows for parental action in varied and enduring ways.

> Theresa (16) refused the requests of her mother, Sila, to be home before midnight during the week. Sila knew that her daughter was deeply attracted to highly problematic kids. Theresa's return late at night led to loud arguments. Sila worried that the neighbors would hear them and call the police. When Theresa became aware of this, she raised her voice

and opened the window. Sila's counselor helped her contact Theresa's two grandmothers and a number of friends and relatives. They all agreed to meet with Theresa in the coming weeks. The supporters were coached to express understanding of Theresa's social needs, but also to assert it was her mother's duty to do all in her power to keep Theresa from harm. In one of those talks Theresa said: "But I can't come home early on weekends!" This signaled the starting point of a negotiation process leading to a compromise. Theresa would be allowed to return later during the weekend, but would have to notify her mother of her whereabouts. On weeknights, she had to be back before midnight. The supporters' continued involvement gradually increased Theresa's willingness to respect the rules. The challenge, however, was not over. After Theresa suddenly stayed out for the whole night, Sila contacted Theresa's friends and talked to some of their parents, as well. She repeated the telephone round two additional times, every time receiving legitimization and help from the supporters. After two months, Sila felt she had an ear to the ground and ways to find and approach Theresa in case of trouble.

Respect and Resistance

Studies that examined adolescents' attitudes regarding parental involvement show that they view actions linked to their safety as legitimate, but actions aimed at disconnecting them from their friends as totally unacceptable (Padilla-Walker, Nelson & Knapp, 2014). We therefore recommend that parents show respect for the child's feelings toward her friends, while resisting tenaciously all damaging and dangerous activities. The parent should openly tell the child that they oppose their damaging relationships, but be aware that the child will probably continue meeting with her friends. They may tell her, for instance: "I understand that you continue meeting with these friends despite my disapproval. I respect your feelings, but my utmost duty is to resist things that put you in danger. I'll watch you closely and get help from others in order to ensure your life is not ruined. I am telling you this frankly, as I know you are loyal to your friends, and my actions might cause them trouble." It is important to say this in a non-threatening way. When parents act this way, they make it more difficult for the child to pursue her dangerous activities. Mentioning the child's loyalty also helps achieve the parents' goal: it shows the child that her parents respect her feelings and see her positive aspects. At the same time, the child's very loyalty obliges her to spare her friends the trouble that might result from the parents' vigilance. In addition, the friends will often blame her for the involvement of her parents and their supporters. This puts a strain on the relationship, sometimes dissolving it altogether.

Gradually, this parental position strengthens the positive voices within the child, which were unable to surface as long as the parents preached, threatened and punished. Loud confrontations usually deafen the positive voices, making the child feel her friends are her only refuge and that her loyalty to them is her supreme duty. In contrast, when the parents stop the confrontations and acknowledge the child's feelings, the emotional atmosphere changes. Parents should not hesitate to express respect for the child's loyalty. Loyalty can be admired, even if it is misplaced. However, the parents should also make it clear that they will resist the child's dangerous involvements. If, however, the parents can accept that the relationship will continue under safer conditions, they should say so just as clearly. Similar messages should reach the child not only from the parents, but also from their supporters and sometimes even from someone within the child's group. These are optimal conditions for the growth of the positive voices in the child's mind. Sometimes the child even signals that, in the depths of her heart, she wishes the parents to continue.

> Maya was worried that her daughter Miv (15) was getting closer to a group of kids, some of whom seemed very problematic in her eyes. At first, she tried to ban the new friendships, but when she saw that this was damaging her relationship with Miv, she opted for a different approach. She went to Miv's room and told her: "I want you to know that I realize that your friends are deeply important to you, and that, emotionally, they're like your second family. I never said this before, as I've come to this understanding only now. I will accept those friendships, if I can also ensure you are not hurt. I want you to know that I'll do all in my power to keep you from drugs, pregnancy, or from getting a sexual disease! If I know you are safe, I'll respect your friendships!" When Miv tried to respond in her usual provocative way, Maya added: "You've never heard me talk like this about the importance of your friendships! And I won't have you wipe out my respectful message to you by screaming it away!" Thereupon she left Miv's room. Later in the day, she wrote the same message to Miv and left it on her bed. This signaled the beginning of a change: Maya intensified her vigilant care and managed, slowly but steadily, to pull Miv away from her most problematic friends.

The Telephone Round[1]

Contacting people with whom the child relates can be a very powerful act. Whenever a parent gains the courage for such a step, he breaks taboo and changes the rules of the game. The child can only be expected to react harshly. Unfortunately, the fear of an outburst deters many parents from taking this step, thus increasing the risk the child is exposed to.

Tony and Gina worried about the new friendships Tino (14) had recently made. But the more they asked, the more Tino would hide his friendships and activities. On one occasion, Tino stayed out very late, and Tony decided to call the mother of one of Tino's friends. Though wakened by the call, she reacted positively and offered Tony her help. Tino returned home right after the call ended. When he found out with whom his father had been speaking, he got into a fury and started throwing things around. He threatened that if they did this again, they would not see him anymore. Tony thought that Tino was about to have a nervous breakdown, and that getting in touch with his friends' parents might make him run away, or worse. Tony and Gina decided not to do it anymore.

These reactions are not rare. Adolescents view their parents' attempt to contact their friends or their parents as an intolerable step. Tino's loss of control can therefore be viewed not only as an impulsive act, but also as an inner decision, a deliberate escalation, meant to deter his parents from repeating their attempt. In effect, the parents did not dare to contact his friends or their parents. The situation, however, went from bad to worse. Tino stopped attending school, stayed out nights and obtained money from unknown sources. If the parents' hope had been that at least their relationship with Tino would be spared, they were badly disappointed, as their relationship reached an all-time low.

Clearly, contacting the child's friends or their parents is an act that requires preparation. The friends' parents should gather a list of phone numbers of people in the child's surroundings in advance. In addition, they should expect a harsh reaction and prepare in advance to absorb the child's attack without responding in kind, while sticking firmly to their duty. The parents should identify themselves and explain why they're calling, for instance: "Our daughter disappeared a couple of times lately, and we're deeply worried about what is happening to her." Friends of the child should be asked to tell their child that they called. Each of these messages is a sign of parental presence. The parents should also try to set up a meeting with the parents of their child's friends who respond positively to their call. Actually talking respectfully with the parents of the child's friends often leads to a positive response. Sometimes parents also receive positive reactions from the child's friends. These friends can be valuable helpers. After a telephone round and a couple of meetings with some of the people contacted, the parents know much more about their child's contacts and activities, are better able to intervene and often gain support for their actions.

When Tony and Gina noticed that Tino's condition continued to deteriorate, and after he was caught with a stolen motorcycle, they decided to recruit a support group, which included not only relatives and friends, but also Tino's soccer coach, two former teachers with whom Tino had had a good relationship, and a known soccer player, whom the parents knew and who proved willing to help. The parents made a number of rounds of phone calls and went twice in person[2] to the street corner where Tino used to hang out with his group. In one of these encounters, the parents got in touch with Ely (16), who showed himself willing to be in touch with them and promised them to look after Tino. Ely told the parents that Tino was under the influence of Eugene, an older youth who hung out on the fringes of their group and was known to be engaged in criminal activities. After two months, Ely succeeded in getting hold of Eugene's address. Escorted by two supporters, Tony went to Eugene's house. He spoke with his parents and told them Tino was only 14 and was under tight supervision. He added that if the relationship between Eugene and Tino continued, he would turn to the police. Tony told them he didn't want to get their son into trouble but that he wouldn't hesitate to do so if it was necessary to rescue Tino. When the father of the elder kid started reacting truculently, Tony repeated politely but firmly that there was no reason for worry, as long as their son kept away from Tino. The parents also managed to contact a couple of other parents whose children were in Tino's group. These parents were concerned about their children too. The other parents agreed to come to a counseling session together with Gina and Tony. Gradually, an agreement regarding curfew and information about where they were staying was reached between the three kids and their parents. Four months later, Tino was still hanging out with the group, but he usually honored the curfew and informed his parents where he was staying. In addition, the dangerous connection with Eugene was broken.

The Child's Inner Voices

The transition from a position of control to a position of supported vigilant care brings about a new balance in the factors influencing the child's behavior. Factors with a negative impact are usually weakened, in favor of more positive ones. Sometimes, an influence that was once deemed purely negative may be revealed as having some positive potential, as when parents succeed in creating an alliance with someone in their child's group. Gradually, the dynamic of inner voices in the child's mind may be tipped in a positive direction. It is important to understand why this is so.

Messages that convey control escalate the conflict. The rebellious teen feels that he must fight back, as complying with the parents' demands means giving up his identity and betraying his friends. Each additional confrontation perpetuates this vicious cycle. After a number of fruitless arguments, the parents start to avoid contact with him. Child and parents begin living parallel lives, in disconnected worlds.

The more the parents act alone, the more cornered and desperate they become. The child, in contrast, feels protected in his group. The parents' world and values become dull and empty in his eyes. Inside the group, in contrast, there is a feeling of vitality and worth.

The situation changes when the parents break out of isolation, cease their controlling messages and engage in vigilant care. Telling the child that they cannot control him, but only themselves, reduces the child's feelings of being under attack. His own attacks against the parents are further reduced when they dare to share their problem with relatives and friends. Involving supporters also helps validate the parents' position. As we all know, some messages are more acceptable to kids when conveyed by persons other than the parents. This is especially true in conflict situations, when the child automatically rejects all parental messages and requests. Supporters, however, may be able to bypass the blocked channel of communication and convey messages in ways that do not result in total rejection. Most adolescents are sensitive to public opinion. Therefore, when the parents' position is relayed by others it leaves a mark, even though they may put up a show of indifference. Moreover, accepting requests posed by the supporters is less humiliating than acceding to the demands of the parents. Supporters thus give the parents broader shoulders. In the eyes of the adolescent, the parents now have a "tribe" of their own. In certain circumstances, he may even consider joining that tribe.

Vigilant care also changes the child's relationship with his group. This happens as group members notice that he is now followed by his parents and their supporters. This may cause unpleasant consequences for the group. If the child wants to be loyal to the group, he should spare them those uncomfortable situations. If he does not reach this conclusion by himself, his friends may make that clear to him.

The balance of influences on the child undergoes further change when the parents contact some of his friends' parents or some of his friends. An alliance between parents may then come into play. When the child's parents or his friends' parents tell him "This is a joint decision that we parents took together!" the child experiences a feeling of greater coherence in his social field. The world the child lives in becomes more continuous. The impact of parental messages grows further if the parents find a friend or two from within the child's group who are also willing to help. We should keep in mind that our child's friends also have different voices in their own minds, and that at least some of them might be willing to help. When we approach them with respect, our chances of reaching those positive voices grow.

The following table summarizes this complex process:

Table 5.1

Processes that occur when the parent acts alone and out of a position of control	Processes that occur when the parent is assisted by supporters and acts out of a position of vigilant care
The child feels a threat to his identity.	The threat on the child's identity is reduced.
Isolation leads the parents to give in or lash back.	Supported parents can stick to their course without lashing back or giving in.
Escalation blocks positive communication and makes the child's actions more extreme.	Confrontations decrease and the gate to positive communication opens.
Isolation reduces the legitimacy of parental acts.	Support strengthens parental legitimacy.
Parental knowledge about the child's connections and activities is minimal.	Parental knowledge about the child's connections and activities grows.
Feelings of loyalty deepen the child's bond with the group.	The child distances himself from the group, out of loyalty, among other reasons.
The group utilizes the difficulties in the parent–child relationship in order to make the child more dependent.	The group distances itself from the child in order to prevent the involvement of the parents and their supporters.
Repetitive confrontations weaken the positive voices in the child's mind.	Decreasing confrontations and the help of supporters strengthen the positive voices in the child's mind.
Disconnection from the parents of the child's friends deepens the gap between the two worlds.	Alliances with parents of friends create a more coherent world.
Disconnection from the child's friends deepens the gap between the two worlds.	Contact with some of the child's friends strengthens vigilant care and reduces the gap between the two worlds.

Notes

1 Detailed instructions for the telephone round and for parental visitations to street corners and other places can be found in Omer (2004).
2 See Omer (2004) for details on parental visitations.

References

Brown, B. B., Bakken, J. P., Ameringer, S. W. & Mahon, S. D. (2008). A comprehensive conceptualization of the peer influence process in adolescence. In M. J. Prinstein & K. A. Dodge (Eds.), *Understanding Peer Influence in Children and Adolescents* (Ch. 2, pp. 17–44). New York: Guilford Press.

Dishion, T. J., Piehler, T. F. & Myers, M. W. (2008). Dynamics and ecology of adolescent peer influence. In M. J. Prinstein & K. A. Dodge (Eds.), *Understanding Peer Influence in Children and Adolescents* (Ch. 4, pp. 72–93). New York: Guilford Press.

Omer, H. (2004). *Non-violent Resistance: A new approach to violent and self-destructive children*. New York and Cambridge: Cambridge University Press.

Padilla-Walker, L. M., Nelson, L. J. & Knapp, D. J. (2014). "Because I'm still the parent, that's why!" Parental legitimate authority during emerging adulthood. *Journal of Social and Personal Relationships*, *31*(3): 293–313.

Segrin, C., Givertz, M., Swaitkowski, P. & Montgomery, N. (2013). Overparenting is associated with child problems and a critical family environment. *Journal of Child and Family Studies*, *24*(2): 470–479.

6 Money

with Yael Nevat and Tal Fisher

Parents often find it difficult to talk with children about money, and not without reason. Almost no family exists that is free from money troubles, or does not have a skeleton in the closet connected to money. There is a popular saying that money has no smell. Nothing could be further from the truth. Money absorbs emotions. There are almost no relationships that are immune to its touch. Entering the world of money is like entering the tangle of life. No wonder parents often prefer to keep their children away from money issues, or at least delay their entrance into this territory.

And yet, age-appropriate discussions about money are vital to prepare children for life (Norvilitis and MacLean, 2010; Kim, Lataillade and Kim, 2011). Avoiding this will only deepen their vulnerability (Marsh, 2006). Money is a key domain of vigilant care, one in which all other risk factors are involved.

But how do we know if the child is mature enough for a first discussion on the topic? Simply put, when the child says, "Buy me that!" or, "I want Johnny's toy too!" he is mature enough. But demands are not the only occasion for talking about money. A visit to the supermarket, buying a present for a friend or going to the movies are good occasions for providing the child with a guided entrance into the world of money (Bowen, 2002).

Parents may dislike the idea of a planned conversation about money, preferring instead that the subject come up by itself. Indeed, one can use everyday occurrences as a cue for this talk. However, if the parents are not prepared in advance and have not taken the trouble to clarify their own position, their reaction may be determined by their emotions rather than the child's needs. Therefore, it is prudent to make a plan for the "money talk," in which the parent explains, guides and inoculates the child against possible risks (Moschis, Moore and Smith, 1984). In the coming chapters, we will read about similar parent-initiated talks about drinking and smoking, the internet or driving. The most notorious of these talks is the one about "the facts of life" (i.e., sexuality), which is the subject of innumerable jokes. The same principle holds in all of these cases: planning ahead allows for a positive interaction, which reduces risk and strengthens parental presence in the child's mind. Relying on spontaneity, in contrast, may lead to poor results.

My parents immigrated to Brazil after the Holocaust. Like many other Jewish immigrants, my father traded in about everything that came to hand. Before immigrating, they lived in Italy, where my father made a living on the black market, which made up practically the whole economy of post-war Italy. In Brazil, he found himself in a similar world, in which the formal economy was only a small parcel of a larger black economy. Many Jews made their living within this reality. The survival skills that were developed in the concentration camps and during their years as refugees allowed them, as strangers in a new land, to make their living. My brother and I grew up in reasonable economic well-being for those times, but the fear of the tax inspector was a constant accompaniment of family life. My parents talked about money only in hushed tones (or in Yiddish, so that we might not understand). I once saw my father taking a hefty amount of bills out of a drawer. I cried out, amazed: "How many thousand cruzeiro bills!" My father responded in anger: "Fool! These are just debts that I have to pay!" I was stunned and slumped. He probably noticed that his reaction was not optimal, for the next day he tried to correct it: "Know that I'm saving money for your future!" He pulled out a thick wad of small bills (of one cruzeiro), and told me: "This is all for you! Every day, if business is good, I add to the pile!" This is how he sought to give me, in his own way, a first idea about savings. I was delighted, and occasionally asked him how my savings were doing. He would reply, "It's growing nicely!" However, one day I deliberately broke a thermometer, just to retrieve the mercury out of it (this was before the age of digital thermometers). My father, probably after a bad day at work, yelled at me: "You'll have to pay for that from your own savings!" I asked him if the thermometer cost a lot. It might have been a good opportunity to instill some first notions about prices and motivate me to take good care of property. Instead, he reacted in anger: "It'll cost all of your savings and the savings that you'll receive for a long time!" In a flick of a wand, all my savings vanished. Not only had I learned nothing about savings, costs and taking care of property, but my feelings that money matters were off limits to me were reinforced, with pretty bad consequences for my future.

There are also problematic reactions at the opposite extreme. For instance, by parents who want to give their child all she wants, perhaps because they suffered from scarcity in their own childhood. Some parents swing between the two poles, trying to create the illusion of no restrictions and reacting harshly when they feel they have gone too far. Thus, my father gave me the illusion of a money wad that inflated miraculously, only to burst the bubble and drain me of all of my fantasized savings in one stroke.

The following two examples are from conversations about money that were initiated by parents with children of different ages.

Bob decided to utilize the occasion of a special show to have an age-appropriate talk with Ike (5) and Eve (8) about prices and priorities:

Eve: Dad, you're going with us to the show?
Bob: I wanted to talk with you about it. Are you sure you want to go?
Eve: Of course, Dad. Why are you asking?
Ike: Yes! Yes!
Bob: Wait, wait, I didn't say we're not going; I just want to know how important it is for you.
Eve: It's very important, all the kids are going!
Ike: Of course! We already have the DVD!
Bob: Is the show so important to you that you'd be willing to give up other things—for example, no candy for a couple of weeks?
Eve: Why?
Bob: The tickets for the show and parking, food and drinks cost money, and when we spend money on one thing, we have less for other things. Imagine the money we have in our family is like beads in a box. The box gets fuller when Mom and I earn money at work, and the box becomes emptier when we buy stuff. In order for us to have enough money for things like food and school for you, we need to set priorities and give up less important things.
Eve: So we're poor? Don't we have enough money?
Bob: We're not poor, but we need to plan our expenses ahead of time. For instance, it is important to me that you have music lessons, and Mom thinks that sports training is important. So we discussed it, and have reached a decision about that. In every family, the parents decide together what is most important, but when dealing with things like this show, you can also participate in the decision. This time, you'll help us decide about the show, and if we choose to go, you'll help us decide what we're saving on, so there's money left for the show.

Liore (16) told her parents that during road safety lessons at school, students were regarded not only as pedestrians but also as drivers, because next year, they would be able to start driving. Gene and Sue decided to take the opportunity to initiate a conversation about their expectations that Liore would save money to help pay for driving lessons:

Gene: We want to talk about how you can contribute to the lessons. Driving will give you a lot of independence! But driving lessons cost a lot of money. And the insurance for young drivers also costs a lot.

Liore: What? You won't pay for my driving lessons?

Sue: It's important for us that you get a license, but we think you should also help. You have another year before you start with the lessons, and you could save up some of the money that you earn from baby-sitting and your summer job.

Liore: That's not fair! You've never asked me to pay for such things!

Gene: That's true, but you are growing up and with more independence comes more responsibility. We can't afford everything all of the time. Your mother and I don't buy everything we want, either. A lot of times, we need to cut expenses and we can't just buy whatever we feel like buying.

Sue: You know that we have some other big expenses this year, like your English summer camp and the orthodontist for you and your sister.

Liore: What's that got to do with it?

Gene: It has to do with it because all of those things come out of the same family fund, which is limited. Whoever feels responsible enough to drive a car should also have other responsibilities. We don't expect you to pay for all of the lessons, but we do expect you to participate. We want to plan this together with you. We want to help with your getting the license, but you'll have to contribute too. We'll talk it over again on Friday. I'm sure we can reach a reasonable solution.

The benefits of these discussions go beyond conveying the basic concepts of money management. They also create a common mental reality, in which the parents are present in the child's mind, and the child in the parents' minds. This is the heart of vigilant care.

To conduct such conversations, parents have to look at their own attitude toward money. This may be the cause for the reluctance some parents feel about those talks. Many parents have weaknesses in their own financial behavior. Promoting responsible money management in the child requires that they make some steps in this direction in their own lives. This does not mean that only parents who set a flawless example can exercise vigilant care. Actually, the parent best suited to guide her child might well be one who is facing difficulties, while making efforts to improve (Norvilitis & MacLean, 2010).

Vigilant care has a "contagious" element, for in order to take care of their child, the parents have to take better care of themselves. Thus, the child is not only the "target" of vigilant care, but becomes a factor that may improve family life. This is not at all uncommon. The experience of parenting makes many of us more responsible in our own lives.

> Andre and Ada heard from their friend Carlos, who took a course on family financial management, that it was important to involve children in talks about money and priorities. Andre and Ada, however, thought their children might respect them less if they knew what troubles they were going through. As the children of both families were already in high school, Carlos suggested inviting the two families together to a lecture on family financial planning. Andre and Ada thought this could help them approach the subject. When the expert talked about the impact of money troubles on the marital and parental relationship, Andre and Ada exchanged embarrassed looks. After the talk, Andre exchanged a few whispered words with his wife and then asked the expert if they could consult with him together with their children about how to improve the family budget.

By showing they are not perfect, but are trying to overcome their limitations, parents may increase the chance the child will learn from their experience. After all, parents who are "only human" are better role models than seemingly perfect ones. One of the central issues of vigilant care is dealing with the child's slip-ups and mistakes. Parents who can model how they struggle to do this in their own lives may then be especially able to help their children.

Withstanding the Child's Inappropriate Demands

The first conversation about money opens an ongoing dialogue that will accompany the child through the years. A basic condition for the success of those talks is that the parents become able to withstand the child's demands ("Buy me that!" "I want it!"). Children who succeed in getting their way by tears or tantrums will not listen to any messages from their parents.

Parents can develop the ability to withstand the child's demands if they set this as an educational priority. Simple answers like, "I have to talk about it with Daddy," or "I'll see whether we can afford this," help check the immediate demand. Support from the other parent or another family member lends the parent additional staying power. Even a very stubborn child ceases to apply pressure when confronted with a parental "No" that is backed by the other parent or the grandparents. Having an open talk with lenient or spoiling grandparents often helps. Even if they protest, they become more willing to check with the parents whether a gift is acceptable or not.

Parents should also prepare themselves for the possibility that the child will circumvent their decision in an unacceptable way. A good preparatory step is to tell the child in advance: "We wll not give in to pressure on this issue. And if by chance you find an unacceptable way to buy this without our permission, we'll cancel the purchase and return the product!" The parent must be prepared for the outrage that may ensue when the purchase is canceled. The readiness to cancel a purchase lends strength to the parents' position, turning them into a potential anchor for situations when the child is exposed to new temptations.

Discussions about the Allowance

Talks about allowance are important periodic events in the parent–child relationship. The allowance is updated as the child grows. The parents' continuous attention to these changes helps them keep an eye on the way the child handles money and on the potential risks to which she is exposed.

> When Dina (13) asked her parents to deposit her allowance in an online account so that she might shop over the net, her parents decided to seize the opportunity to teach her how to manage her money. Together with Dina, they sought an appropriate internet site for her age. They discussed the products that she was allowed to buy and formulated basic rules regarding purchases. They also found a site on sensible consumer behavior that was suitable both for Dina and for them. During their joint introduction to the new field, they realized that Dina could help them with market surveys and price comparisons for products that the family needed. Dina's request thus turned into an important event, which allowed the whole family to improve their consumer habits.

Money that the child receives or earns provides good opportunities for conversations (Kim, LaTaillade & Kim, 2011; Bowen, 2002). Parents should ask the child about her wishes, define legitimate expenses and make it clear that they expect the child to get their permission for any important purchase. The child is also asked to discuss with them any loan requests to or from friends. Those talks define rules, strengthen parental presence in the child's mind and increase parental knowledge.

Events like a parent's temporary unemployment or illness, special medical expenses or preparation for a joint holiday may be the occasion for a serious talk. Sometimes the talk is about something that happened to someone else.

> *Roy:* I've heard that Debby can't go on the scouts' trip because her mother had twins and stopped working, so they don't have enough money!
> *Mom:* What does Debby say about it?
> *Roy:* She mentioned it is as if she didn't mind. But I saw how sorry she was. It's awful! That trip is the major social event of the year! She will end up all alone!
> *Mom:* Aren't you exaggerating?

> *Roy:* Not at all! We'll all have shared experiences that she won't know about, jokes that she won't understand; in short, she'll feel left out.
>
> *Mom:* Sounds like a real issue, but what would you do if we had less money? Last year, Dad had to leave his job and didn't get a new one for five months. We were on the verge of making serious cuts in the family budget. We would then also have to give up on some important things. Debby's family have to reduce their income for some time so that Debby's mother can take care of the twins. Debby probably understands that. She's your friend, and this may be a time when you can stand by her. Maybe you and your friends can do something so that she doesn't feel left out.

Many parents prefer to spare their children exposure to money issues, perhaps to keep them free from worries for a few more years. However, in trying to maintain their children in a money-free paradise, they may actually be creating a fool's paradise. In contrast, some families succeed in having positive talks about money even with relatively young children:

> Gene and Irma decided they would limit their weekly spending at the supermarket to 100 dollars. It was clear that the cut would affect some of their usual purchases. Gene, who sometimes took Nina (8) with him to the supermarket, told her about the limit they had imposed on themselves. He showed her how he arranged the products in the trolley in order of importance. When they came to the cash register, they passed the necessary products first and only then, as they saw they were still 20 dollars below budget, started passing the other products. Gene told Nina that once the bill at the register reached the 100-dollar limit, they would stop and leave the other products behind. When the bill reached 102 dollars, he asked Nina if she wanted to decide which product should be left at the store. Nina did not hesitate: she chose a bag of snacks that she usually enjoyed and suggested that they leave it out. The total purchase dropped to 97 dollars. Nina smiled proudly at her father.

As the child grows, so too grows her independence in managing her personal budget. However, at least as long as the child lives at home, this should match the family's values and needs.

> Rick (19) had developed a daily routine that made his parents more and more worried. He slept late, spent many hours at the computer and almost never took part in the household chores. He earned enough

money to fulfill his needs through his computer programming skills. Those freelance jobs demanded from him only a few hours of work each week. When his parents asked him about his plans, Rick told them that at the moment that style of life suited him well. When this situation continued for over two years, the parents decided to take action. They told Rick that they wanted to talk to him about his participation in the household costs and chores. They told him they had to redefine their mutual responsibilities. To Rick's surprise, his parents presented him with a list of household expenses, social security, medical insurance, car expenses and internet services that he was costing them. They also presented him with a list of services he was used to receiving from them. They then asked him to think how he was going to contribute to the costs and chores. Rick asked provokingly: "You want me to pay you rent?" They answered him calmly: "You have to participate in your costs and household duties!" Rick didn't answer and for a while tried to avoid meeting with his parents. He bought himself a car with the money he had earned and announced that he would no longer use the family car. His parents told him that they saw this as a positive step. A few weeks after their initial talk, they came to him again and told him: "You haven't made any suggestions as to how you're going to contribute to the family budget and chores. Therefore, we made up a list ourselves." They presented a summary of expenses, and told him what they expected from him on a monthly basis. They also told him that they expected him to buy groceries once a week for the whole family (they would share the costs), to stop eating in his room, to take the dog out for walks and be responsible for cleaning the table after they ate. Rick reacted more positively this time. He started to contribute a fixed sum for household expenses, and after two months said he wanted to go to college. The parents said they would finance his tuition and part of his living expenses, as they had done for his sister. Until he left, Rick continued contributing to the household expenses and chores.

Dealing with Harmful Financial Behavior

Vigilant care transitions to the highest level when clear warning signs appear. Some typical examples are: the child demands more and more money, creates debts, gambles, buys friends with presents, steals, or obtains money or objects from unexplained sources. All of these point to potentially serious entanglements. Thus, when the parents exercise vigilant care over their child's problematic financial behavior, they widen their view over their child's potential troubles, and become better able to take protective action when needed.

Talking about money can be particularly helpful, because the parents can then ask precise and focused questions that are often more difficult in other areas. The reason is that in the financial domain, they can use the good services of arithmetic. If the child's explanations do not add up, there are omissions or falsity in the report. Financial behavior is thus especially suitable for creating transparency. However, many parents avoid a pointed discussion, even though they see the writing on the wall.

> At 15, I started working at my parents' tobacco shop in São Paulo, which was managed by Abraham, my mother's cousin. I used to take over his shift every day at noon for two hours (I attended an evening school). According to the agreement, I received 50 cruzeiros a day for my work. I took the money directly from the cash register. Abraham loved me, and we had a close and equal relationship that went far beyond what might be expected in light of the generation gap between us. This fact might have contributed to his turning a blind eye to the fact that I didn't just settle for the agreed sum, but also took some added compensation, both in the form of cigarettes and additional money that I allowed myself without reporting to him. I deluded myself into thinking that my thefts went unnoticed because Abraham had never called me out on them. My parents also never asked questions, trusting that Abraham would keep an eye on me. Two years after I had started working at the store, Abraham shattered this illusion when he gave me a strong hint that he knew exactly how much money was missing from the till. I was ashamed and stopped taking money (although I kept stocking up on cigarettes). Throughout the years, I wondered how this systematic disregard might have affected my life. I believe it added to my uncontrolled attitude toward money, which characterized my financial behavior during my early years as an adult and parent. In addition, there were also clear dangers into which I could have stumbled. I had a friend a few years older than me who got into trouble with debt and embezzled money from the travel agency where he worked. He told me of a sophisticated ploy by which he thought he would be able to repay his debts, and more. He asked me to help him with a sum of money that he needed in order to execute his scheme. Fortunately, this occurred right after Abraham had made it clear to me that he knew about the missing money from the till. If it hadn't been for that, I might well have agreed to help my friend get out of his mess, probably getting into a deep mess of my own.

When parents become aware that the child has trouble with money, they have to raise the issue openly. A good way to open up the conversation is to tell the child: "We know that you're getting in trouble with money. We want to talk to you so as best to help you stop whatever is leading you into trouble!" Such a message may help the child cooperate as it shows that the parents are acting out of love and concern.

A major goal of the conversation is to create transparency, which raises the level of vigilant care and helps promote responsible management. This is true not only with children and adolescents, but also with an adult child who got entangled in debt and requires help from his parents.

Roy (27) was entirely dependent on his parents financially. He lived in an apartment they bought for him, and they paid for all his expenses. In the past, Roy used to work and had shown himself able to keep a job. He had a talent for interpersonal contact and created good relations with clients. However, he had always dreamed of becoming an actor, and his parents decided to allow him to pursue his dream. He was accepted by a reputable school, but dropped out in the first year. He tried to get into another school, but didn't pass the auditions. After this, he didn't go back to work, and his parents continued to give him the same monthly sum as when he was studying. However, there were clear signs that, aside from the fact that Roy wasn't working, the money they gave him wasn't enough for him anymore. The situation deteriorated and he asked for their help, after receiving notice from the bank that his credit card was going to be blocked. The parents decided they had to achieve full transparency, but Roy refused to disclose his accounts, arguing that this information was personal. The parents told him they were willing to seek the help of a professional, who would go through his accounts with him and help him prepare a financial plan. They told him they were willing to help him, but only under professional supervision and with a fully transparent and organized plan. The financial counselor would provide the parents with summarized reports that would not specify the personal contents of Roy's expenses. He agreed to the parents' terms, and collaborated with the financial counselor. Roy started working, and though he changed jobs a few times, he didn't stay unemployed for long. A year later, he had repaid most of his debts and returned some of the money that his parents had given him to keep him afloat. After a couple of relatively stable years, the parents were tempted to give Roy a gift (for his 30th birthday), so that he would be able to fulfill his dream of visiting London to watch theater performances. To their astonishment, the trip to London ended with new debts, threatening to destroy Roy's hard-won stability. The parents re-hired the financial counselor. The event made it clear to them that they had to be very careful of any situation where Roy could enjoy their financial services in an unsupervised way.

Gil (15) had expensive hobbies. He demanded to receive the money from his Bar-Mitzvah, spending most of it on his stamp collection. Later, he fell in love with electronic gadgets. He sold his stamp collection and started to buy and sell gadgets over the web. Then his parents discovered that he had started gambling. He had sold all his devices to purchase gambling forms on soccer games. He neglected his studies and focused compulsively on the games' results. He started to accumulate debts with his friends. Two months after the parents found out about the gambling and the debts, Gil's grandmother told the parents that he had come to her in tears, begging for money to repay a friend. He promised it would never happen again, and made her swear that she wouldn't tell them. The grandmother gave him the money and kept the secret, but when the parents told her about Gil's gambling, she revealed the incident. The parents told their son that they knew about the debts, the money he'd gotten from his grandmother and the gambling. They told him they were going to keep a close eye on him and would contact anyone who could help save him from the gambling. Gil's father and his brother went together to two places where Gil used to buy gambling forms. The sellers promised that they would not sell him any more forms in the future. The father also spoke with some of Gil's friends, and told them that he was at high risk of becoming addicted to gambling. Most of the friends responded positively, and told the father they would not cooperate with Gil's purchasing of gambling forms or any other gambling activities. The parents gathered the extended family for a meeting, shared their problem with them and asked everyone not to comply with any of Gil's demands for money. At the meeting, it turned out he had also managed to receive money from his other grandmother and had asked for loans from two older cousins. The parents announced to Gil they would make periodic checks in his room and bags. The situation appeared to calm down. Two years later, they found a gambling form in his room and understood that he was gambling again. They confronted Gil and resumed their supervision. The parents now knew that Gil was at serious risk of becoming an addictive gambler. Though they had succeeded in getting him reasonably clean through the end of high school, they were not at all sure about what the future would bring. In any case, any untoward developments would not catch them unprepared.

References

Bowen, C. F. (2002). Financial knowledge of teens and their parents. *Journal of Financial Counseling and Planning*, *13*(2), 93.

Kim, J., LaTaillade, J. & Kim, H. (2011). Family processes and adolescents' financial behaviors. *Journal of Family and Economic Issues*, *32*(4), 668–679.

Marsh, B. A. (2006). Examining the personal finance attitudes, behaviors, and knowledge levels of first-year and senior students at Baptist universities in the state of Texas (Doctoral dissertation, Bowling Green State University).

Moschis, G. P., Moore, R. L. & Smith, R. B. (1984). The impact of family communication on adolescent consumer socialization. In Thomas C. Kinnear (Ed.), *NA-Advances in Consumer Research, Volume 11*. Provo, UT: Association for Consumer Research. (pp. 314–319)

Norvilitis, J. M. & MacLean, M. G. (2010). The role of parents in college students' financial behaviors and attitudes. *Journal of Economic Psychology*, *31*(1), 55–63.

7 Cigarettes, Alcohol and Drugs

*with Tal Carty, Dan Solomon and
Avigail Hirsch-Asa*

In order to exercise vigilant care regarding a specific risk factor, parents should begin by staging a preparatory talk on the subject with the child. The goals of this talk are: (a) to raise the child's awareness about the risk factor and the parents' stance and concern regarding it; (b) to increase the parents' presence in the child's mind; and (c) to facilitate communication on the subject.

The preparatory talk is intended as a kind of rite of passage, that is, an event that marks a transition between one condition in life and another, in this case a transition from a time when the risk factor was not yet viewed as relevant to the child to one when it is. The child is thus viewed as "growing up" into new kinds of risk. In this chapter, we illustrate how such talks can be initiated, conducted and followed-up, illustrating this with the subject of tobacco, drug and alcohol use.

In every culture, important life transitions are signaled by rites of passage. Those rites become registered in the minds of all participants, creating a break in the continuous flow of time. Rites of passage may be highly formal, such as those that signal a new condition in life—for instance, first communion, bar-mitzvah or marriage—or less formal—for instance, handing over the car keys to a new driver or shaking hands to signal a mutual commitment. Rites of passage are also helpful to stop a negative habit, such as quitting smoking (Suarez, 2012).

All parents want their children to be protected against the abuse of substances. If there was a recipe that guaranteed total inoculation of their child against those risks, most would probably be willing to adopt it. Such a recipe, of course, does not exist. Parents often ask us: "How can we guarantee that our child won't touch those substances?" We have no answer to this question. All we can say is that the risk will be lower if the child feels that the parents are present in her life and accompany her as closely as necessary.

Many parents are surprised that a peremptory statement like, "I absolutely forbid you to smoke!" or, "Drugs are totally out of bounds!" does not further vigilant care, but rather tends to block communication, as the child will keep silent if and when she is exposed to those substances. However, when parents make their position clear, in less authoritarian ways, they definitely reduce risk

(Chassin et al., 2005). It thus pays to have a preparatory talk, but parents should conduct it with a mind to keeping communication open.

> My father had declared threateningly that I should never touch a cigarette under any circumstances. However, this was insufficient to counter the social pressure of my friends. When we watched, in utter dismay, how the legendary Pelé massacred our team in the stadium of São Paulo, and my friends offered me a cigarette in consolation, or at least to put up a show of courageous fraternity in the face of adversity, I could not refuse. After this initiation, I continued smoking on special occasions, hiding it of course from my parents. The addictive process was quick: when I was 14, I already smoked a pack a day and worked to pay for my habit. My parents found me out only when I was 19. The only effect of my father's threat was to make me more secretive.

The meetings of teenagers are characterized by a special atmosphere that dampens the parents' voices. The majority of youngsters probably begin smoking as part and parcel of their group experience. Parents cannot expect their voice to be always stronger than the voice of the group. After all, growing peer influence is one of the normative processes of adolescence. However, even if the parents' voice in the child's mind does not block each and every temptation, its echo may dampen the extent of compliance or help their child pull herself together later on.

Parents rank the degree of danger they attribute to different substances differently. However, the similarities in the reasons why kids begin using them and the goals they serve (e.g., feeling part of the group, or getting into "the right state of mind") justify including them all in the same preparatory talk.

The parents' first goal in this conversation is to increase the likelihood that their child will think about them when she is exposed to temptation. The goal is not necessarily to convert the child to the parents' attitude. Children who tend to be convinced will be convinced; others, less so. However, the talk's success is not only measured by the conviction it produces, but is also a function of the mental accompaniment it creates. Even if the child does not identify fully with the parents' position, an important goal will be achieved if she remembers the parents at the moment of trial. Moreover, the conversation puts the subject on the family agenda, legitimizing the parents' continuing attention.

Before conducting the talk, the parents should check that they are in agreement. This is not always an easy task. One of the parents may be skeptical about the usefulness of such talks, thinking the child will do her own thing anyhow or even do the exact opposite of what the parents want. In such situations, the more decided parent should conduct the talk on her own. The prospect is better when the other parent is willing to show some degree of support, for instance, by telling the child that the conversation takes place with his agreement. If even this modest level of cooperation cannot be achieved, the active parent may ask the other not to contradict her position or engage in critical remarks. This request may be more effective if made by a third party, for instance, a family friend whom the other parent respects. Fortunately, even parents who tend to be divided on other issues usually agree that substance abuse is dangerous. Thus, at least some cooperation can usually be achieved.

Parents who are smokers experience obvious difficulties in expressing to their child a position that is subverted by their own behavior. When one parent does not smoke, he or she should conduct the conversation (van der Vorst Engels, Meeus & Dekovic, 2006). If both parents smoke, it may be better to find someone whom the child respects to have the conversation with the child in their place. The supporter will conduct the talk in the parents' absence. But it is helpful to say: "I am talking with you about this with your parents' knowledge and agreement. They thought that it would be best that they do not conduct this conversation, as both of them are smokers. However, this fact does not invalidate their deep wish that you don't fall victim to their habit!"

A quasi-formal talk is better than a casual one. The actual talk may be prefaced by a declaration like: "You are now at an age when we have to talk with you about cigarettes, alcohol and drugs. Let's set up a date when we can talk undisturbed." In this way, the conversation is marked as a special event that stands out from the flow of ordinary interactions. The parents can add: "This will be a special conversation: regardless of what you may tell us, we promise not to threaten you or get angry. An open conversation on those matters is very important for us!" The talk can take place in the living room, a coffee house or the parent's office. Cell phones should be turned off. These are, of course, artificial steps. We should, however, keep in mind that getting a vaccine against polio is artificial too, and yet it is a highly efficient preventive step.

The parents should ask the child if he's already been exposed to any of those substances. Questions like, "Are there kids who smoke at school?" "Was there alcohol at any of the parties you attended?" may bring informative answers. If the child says he did not notice anything, the parents may add: "This hasn't yet happened, but it surely will. You will come across situations in which some of your friends will smoke or drink, and will offer you cigarettes or alcohol or even try to convince you to join them." When this parental prediction comes true, the child will probably remember the parents' words. This creates a mental bridge between the conversation and the moment of temptation.

> Rose invited her daughter Sybil (13) to a coffee shop to have an open talk about smoking and drinking. She said this was a good time to have this talk, as Sibyl was beginning to party and was about to go to summer camp. The following exchange ensued:
>
> *Rose:* Do any of your friends smoke or drink?
> *Sibyl:* No, but there are two boys who go out in the middle of the party, sort of boasting they're going to smoke.

Rose: If someone offered you a cigarette, how would you react?
Sibyl: Mom, my friends are not like that!
Rose: I'm glad to hear that! I want you to feel that your dad and I stand behind you, so as to give you strength not to give in to social pressure to smoke or drink alcohol, when and if this happens.

Rose felt that would be enough as a first talk. It was short, but opened up communication on the subject.

Vera and Martin, parents of Steve (14), feared that their son would immediately rebuff them at the start of the conversation. Martin said to him: "We want to have an open talk with you about cigarettes, alcohol and drugs. I know that you hate when we interrogate you or preach to you, so I want to say right off the bat that we are not going to do that. We want to have a short and positive talk. I know that tonight you're going bowling. We want to sit with you before you leave." This is how the actual talk developed:

Steve: I'm already late, I don't have time!
Martin: It won't be long. This talk is very important for us.
Steve: So make it quick!
Martin: Let's turn off our cellphones so we won't be disturbed and the talk will be quicker.
Steve: Why are you making such a fuss? None of my friends do drugs!
Martin: I'm glad to hear that! But we want to talk with you anyhow, and not especially about drugs, but also about cigarettes and alcohol. We promise that we won't get angry, no matter what you tell us. Do any of your friends smoke or drink?
Steve: If they did, do you think I'd tell you?
Martin: I don't think so! I know that you're loyal to your friends. I won't ask you to give me any special information. But I'd like to ask you how you'd react if they offered you some.
Steve: Quit it! That's enough, OK?
Martin: This talk is important to us, and I know that it is unpleasant for you. But we'd be pretty bad parents if we did not try to keep you safe. When you're with your friends, you are alone with them, we're not there with you. We're glad you're enjoying yourself, but we're worried too, and we'd like to believe that you'd be able to say "No!" I'd be proud to know that you're strong enough not to be a sucker when friends put pressure on you.

Steve: I'm nobody's sucker! Mom, you're sitting there silently. Is this all Dad's idea?

Vera: No, we're in this together. I'm glad you said you're nobody's sucker! I'd be very happy if you'd remember that when somebody offers you grass or alcohol.

Steve: I've told you that I don't intend to get addicted!

Martin: I don't think anyone ever intended to get addicted. People try alcohol or drugs out of curiosity or because they want to belong. The first time is like that, but pretty quickly it becomes something else.

Steve: I hate the smell of cigarettes!

Martin: Wonderful! That protects you! If you didn't hate the smell, you'd be in more danger.

Steve: No way!

Martin: And what about grass? Someone will surely offer you some, and tell you how great it is! Or someone will bring a bottle of vodka that he stole from his parents and offer to have a party before the party.

Steve nodded, showing he knew what they were talking about. That was a good moment to end the conversation.

Steve: It's clear that you know what we're talking about. I promised we wouldn't push, be angry or threaten. So let's stop here. If you get into such a situation, think about us. We think about you all the time!

Parents often react angrily at the child's lack of respect, thus diverting the conversation from its goal. If they understand that this is precisely the child's aim in his cutting answers, they may be better able to withstand the provocations and lead the conversation in the desired direction. By doing so, they put the subject on the family agenda and show they are vigilant. Parents can end the conversation by saying: "When someone offers you cigarettes, alcohol or drugs, we won't be there with you! Only your friends will be there. But now we are with you, so we want to tell you how we feel about the matter. To tell you the truth, we hope that when you're with your friends, you'll remember us!" This conclusion creates a bridge between the conversation and the temptation. This is precisely the parents' goal.

Here are some additional messages that parents gave their children in different circumstances. Parents can choose which ones match their style, beliefs and values:

"I hope you won't touch those substances. I hope you'll be strong enough to resist the pressure to try them. I want to tell you that I was very proud of you when you refused to participate in the attack against Victor, even though some of your friends were part of it!"

> "There are kids who drink alcohol or smoke grass to feel more socially at ease. But then their ability to function socially without those substances decreases. That's precisely what is called 'dependence.' If you feel that you also have to do that in order to relax, remember that we are here to help you find better solutions."
>
> "The first cigarette is almost always unpleasant. The process whereby you turn the unpleasant experience into a pleasant one is the process of becoming addicted. The moment you enjoy cigarettes, addiction has set in. Alcohol is different: it may lead to an immediate feeling of pleasure and relaxation. However, when you use it again and again, you want it more and more. This is addiction."

Ending the conversation on a positive note creates the best chance to protect the child in the real situation. Here is a conclusion that summarizes all the main points:

> "We started this talk so that you may think about us and weigh your reaction when you are confronted with such situations. We have no doubt that events like these will occur. We hope you won't accept the offer, but if this ever happens or has already happened, we hope it will remain an isolated event. It is very important to us that you feel you can turn to us, tell us what is happening and think with us how best to cope. We wanted you to know that we care for you and keep our eyes open so that nothing bad happens to you!"

The preparatory talk sets the stage for parents to raise the subject. Any new kind of social event or change in the child's social routine can justify raising the subject again. A very short talk will then suffice. Parents are afraid that if they raise the subject again, the child will become more resistant. The parents can then say: "If you're tired of my harping on this because you feel you're strong enough to withstand the temptation, I'm glad of that!"

When the parents notice that the child is probably drinking or smoking, they should intensify their vigilant care.

> Helen knew that her son Michael (16) was smoking regularly. The smell of smoke when she came near him betrayed him, but when she asked him,

he answered evasively. After a while, the smell of cigarettes was replaced by the smell of chewing gum. Beforehand he didn't chew gum at all. She searched his room and found a pack of cigarettes. She discussed this with her husband, Mario, and they decided to have a talk with Michael. After agreeing on their position, they entered his room together and asked him to shut off the computer for a moment. Mario, who had more authority than Helen and was closer to Michael, led the conversation:

Michael: What's the matter?
Mario: We have a serious matter to discuss with you. We know that you smoke, and we want to have an open talk about it.
Michael: I don't smoke regularly. I tried a couple of times when friends offered me a cigarette.
Mario: We don't think so. There are many signs that you're smoking frequently, and I think it's better that instead of arguing we think together about a solution.
Micheal: What do you want?
Mario: We want you to stop.
Michael: OK.
Mario: How will you do that?
Michael: I'm not a regular smoker, I smoke only here and there. So I'll just stop.
Mario: I believe in your good will. But I'd be glad to get a more serious answer from you, an answer that would increase our trust.
Michael: So what do you expect me to say?
Mario: I'll be glad if you commit yourself seriously to stop smoking. This will be a step in the right direction. And we'll keep an eye out, because lately there were clear signs that you were hiding your smoking. Another thing: I'd be glad if you told your friends that you quit smoking. Are you willing to think together with me how to do that?
Michael: No problem, I can tell them right away!
Mario: Excellent! Are you willing to send them an SMS now? That would make us feel a lot better.
Michael: OK!

This exchange was possible because of the positive relationship between Michael and his father. The parents' self-control was crucial to the conversation's success. The parents could not know for sure if their son would keep his promise. But the conversation increased the likelihood that Michael would feel his parents mentally present. His readiness to notify his friends, and his feeling that he was increasing his parents' trust, reduced the risk to some extent.

Clara knew that her daughter Eva (17) smoked. She had tried to talk with her about it a number of times in the past, but Eva had rebuffed her. Being divorced, Clara asked her friend Nina, who had a good relationship with Eva, to help her. Nina invited Eva to go with her to a cafe.

Nina: Your mother told me that you smoke, and I volunteered to help because we have a good relationship and I know that you won't lie to me.
Eva: All of my friends smoke!
Nina: You don't want to quit?
Eva: No, I tried a couple of times, but I couldn't.
Nina: If you want, I can take you to someone who helps people stop smoking.
Eva: The truth is that now is not the right time for me.
Nina: You can talk to me about it whenever you feel you want to. But you should know that your mother will not pay for your habit.
Eva: What do you mean?
Nina: She'll reduce your allowance so that she won't feel she's paying for cigarettes. If you behave offensively to her, she'll probably also reduce other services, such as your smartphone account.
Eva: She wouldn't dare!
Nina: I think you're wrong! I talked to her, and she has already talked about it with your dad. They decided that you're a big girl, and that if you want to smoke, you'll have to pay for it. To tell you the truth, I think they're right.
Eva: I want to see if they dare to do that!

To Eva's surprise, Clara told her that same evening about the reduction in her allowance. Eva started screaming and threatening. Clara ended the conversation and called Eva's father. He phoned Eva half an hour later and told her that he agreed with Clara's decision and said he would also reduce his contribution to her allowance. He told her that if she were willing to reconsider taking part in a program to stop smoking, he would also reconsider.

With Nina's mediation, a compromise was reached, but only after Eva had her allowance curtailed for two months. Thereupon, she agreed to go for treatment to stop smoking. The parents renewed her allowance, but told her they would keep their finger on the pulse. Clara and George knew full well there was no guarantee that Eva would stop smoking, or even that she would seriously try to do so. But the parents' steps strengthened their position and showed Eva that they were willing to join hands on issues regarding her health. At the very least, Eva's participation in the treatment might strengthen her wish to stop smoking and give her some tools that she might use if and when she decided to do so. Those are modest results, but vigilant care is not control.

Dolly, Bill's (16) widowed mother, watched helplessly as he became more and more involved with pot. She allowed him to smoke in his room, out of fear that he would be driven to worse places. Bill woke up late every morning, and missed school more and more often. He would invite his friends to smoke in his room, and they would sometimes stay over until the morning. Bill's room became the pot center of the neighborhood. With the help of a counselor from our center, Dolly gathered a support group that included relatives, friends and the parents of a close friend of Bill's. She declared to Bill, verbally and in writing, that she would no longer agree to him smoking in the house. She demanded that his door remain unlocked at all times. She declared she would fight the drugs and their effect on his life by any means possible, and with the help of anyone willing to support her. With the help of her support group, she also conveyed the new house rules to some of the friends who used to come and smoke in Bill's room. The supporters told Bill's friends that Bill would be under close supervision, and that Dolly would not hesitate to call the police if there was a grass party in his room. Bill reacted by saying he would protect his privacy rights, and declared an immediate school-strike. Dolly knew that Bill would try to blackmail her in this manner. She knew that Bill's presence at school was at best formal and that the chances he would pass his exams were slim. On the first day of his strike, she told him that she would stop all the special services he received from her. One of the supporters called him to back her decision. Two other supporters helped Dolly disconnect Bill's computers and the TV. She canceled Bill's smartphone account and his allowance. The supporters helped her make a telephone round in which she notified Bill's friends and their parents of her decision. When Bill left the house she searched his room and found a bong and some hash. She threw everything away. When Bill returned, his 26-year-old cousin, Jeff, was waiting in his room. He told Bill that he had helped his mother throw away the drugs and the bong. He told Bill that all the people in the group cared for him and believed he could overcome his problem. The parents of Bill's friends who took part in the support group visited the house and left a message for Bill, telling him that they had instituted the same rules in their homes. In the following days, seven people visited the house or contacted Bill by phone or e-mail. When he refused to answer, they left him a message. They all offered their help to Bill, and said that Dolly had to act that way in order to save him from the drugs. A week later, Jeff invited Bill to stay with him at his apartment for a few days. Bill was glad to go. It was clear to Dolly and to all the supporters that at home, Bill would find it especially hard to make a positive step. The situation, however, might be different if he stayed with Jeff. Any change he might undertake there would not be perceived as capitulation to his mother's pressure. Bill stayed at Jeff's house for a month and, during this time, he started to go to school again. Jeff helped him with math, a subject in which Bill had good chances of succeeding. Jeff also found him a private tutor to help him prepare himself for some of his other exams. Two days after Bill returned to school, Jeff told him his smartphone account and allowance were being renewed. Jeff invited Bill's friend (whose parents were in the support group) to the apartment and the two got help together to prepare for their exams. Dolly knew that Bill probably continued smoking grass, but now his life was no longer dominated by it. Jeff kept in touch with Bill and his friend over the summer. Having a friend take part in the process and having an "older brother" (Jeff) involved made things more acceptable for Bill. But the key factor had been the change that took place in Dolly's heart.

References

Chassin, L., Persson, C. C., Rose, J., Sherman, S. J., Davis, M. J. & Gonzalez, J. L. (2005). Parenting style and smoking-specific parenting practices as predictors of adolescent smoking onset. *Journal of Pediatric Psychology*, *30*, 333–344.

Suarez, M. (2012). Cigarette abandonment and rituals: Understanding smoking cessation symbolism. Rio de Janeiro: UFRJ/COPPEAD.

van der Vorst, H., Engels, C. M. E., Meeus, W. & Dekovic, M. (2006). The impact of alcohol-specific rules, parental norms about early drinking and parental alcohol use on adolescents' drinking behavior. *Journal of Child Psychology and Psychiatry*, *47*, 1299–1306.

8 Computers and the Internet

with Yaron Sela

Problematic Internet Use (PIU) refers to utilization of the internet in ways that cause difficulties in mental health, interpersonal relationships and scholastic domains (Shapira et al., 2003). One of the most vulnerable populations is adolescents. Epidemiological data show that rates range from 2%–10% in Europe (Kormas et al., 2011), 4% in the US (Liu et al., 2011) and 18%–30% in Southeast Asian countries (Wang et al., 2011). Extremely high rates led China and South Korea to identify PIU as a major public health threat (Cash, Rae, Steel & Winkler, 2012).

The risks to which adolescents are exposed have been divided into three categories: content, contact and commercial (De Moor et al., 2008). Content risk refers to sites containing pornography, propagating damaging behaviors like drug use, anorexia or suicide or glorifying violent behaviors. Contact risk refers to potentially dangerous interactions, the most notorious of which is contact with pedophiles. Adolescents often share personal information with people they do not know. This makes them vulnerable to pedophiles and other predators (Livingstone, 2006). In addition, children who self-expose in blogs or social networks incur the risk that the exposure may cause damage or be used against them. Another risk is cyber-bullying, a distressful experience with potentially disastrous consequences (Kowalski, Giumetti, Schroeder & Lattanner, 2014). Commercial risk results from adolescents being easy prey for marketing techniques designed to turn them into active consumers. In their eagerness, children sometimes supply their parents' credit cards, with or without the parents' knowledge.

Parents don't have to be well versed in the secrets of the internet to start protecting their children and themselves. Being acquainted with this list and with some principles of vigilant care may help them increase their child's safety.

Though parents can be an important buffer against PIU (Williams & Merten, 2011), they face special difficulties in trying to set limits regarding the computer or smartphone. Parents often feel much less competent than their children in this area. Children are "digital natives," while their parents are "digital immigrants" (Palfrey & Gasser, 2013). Moreover, despite its risks and hazards, the internet also offers important advantages. Parents are thus in a dilemma: how to keep the positive while preventing the negative. In addition, parental involvement may meet with strong resistance from the child. These difficulties lead many parents to leave the child to himself in his virtual world.

Many parents would be surprised to hear that in a relatively short time it is possible to develop vigilant care skills that can reduce their helplessness and the child's risk. In our pilot project on the subject, we have shown that a few hours of training may suffice to help parents feel more knowledgeable, involved and capable of intervening when necessary (Alexandron, 2012; Geyra, 2011; Nataneli, 2013).

Parents should understand that the hope to achieve control over the child's activities in the virtual world is illusory. Control is impossible because, among other reasons, the virtual world is so easily accessible. Children can get access not only from their computer or smartphone, but also at their friends' houses, or even at school. Trying to block all of those possibilities is literally impossible. However, the parents can exercise vigilant care, allowing them to function as a lighthouse, a safety net and an anchor. Their role then is not to control, but to safeguard. This attitude has a profound advantage over the attempt to achieve control, in that vigilant care leads to less conflict, is more legitimate and fosters the development of self-care.

Parents can create a good platform for vigilant care over the child's virtual activities through a preparatory conversation, similar to what we described regarding cigarettes, alcohol and drugs. However, in contrast to the initial talk about substance abuse, which is usually quite short, the interchange regarding the virtual world can take a couple of hours. We also propose that parents and child sign a contract regarding safe use of the computer and the smartphone. Signing a contract is fitting for this domain (as it is for driving as well, as shown below), because in those areas the parents offer the child a special service (computer, smartphone and internet) that can also be misused. When a service with potential risk is purveyed, it is fit to make that service conditional on the user's commitment to safe use. Moreover, the contract legitimizes the parents in intensifying vigilant care when the child does not keep his commitment. The contract also increases the chances that the child will remember the parents when confronted with situations that are specified in it.

The preparatory talk may begin with one or both of the parents requesting that the child give them a "guided tour" on the computer and smartphone. The parents can say: "For us, the internet is a new world. So we want to ask you to give us a guided tour and show us the games, sites and activities you engage in with the smartphone and computer. This is not an investigation! You are free to show me what you want! We won't nudge or grill you!"

The better the parents understand that conducting the talk is part of their basic duty to protect the child, the more they will radiate decisiveness. They can then make their request quietly, but with self-assurance. In the majority of cases, the child cooperates. If she refuses, this is in itself an alarm sign, indicating that in all likelihood she is using the internet in unacceptable ways. This would justify transitioning to a higher level of vigilant care.

Parental interest in the child's games and other activities often creates a positive atmosphere. A very general description like "I play role-playing games" is not sufficient. The parents should ask for examples, and really try to understand. In the process, they often discover that the child has skills of which they were unaware. Most children will be surprised by the parents' interest. Many enjoy this interaction, particularly if they feel the parents are motivated by genuine curiosity. Studies found that communicating with children about the internet, and spending time online together, increases adolescents' sense of safety, and decreases the risk for PIU (Liu et al., 2012).

The parents can also ask the child to show them his Facebook page. If the child hesitates, the parents can suggest that if the child wants to make some changes before he shows them the page, it is OK with them. In this way, they show they are motivated by positive interest and not by an investigative frame of mind. Indeed, the purpose of the guided tour is not to discover any problematic activities, but to create a positive parental presence in the child's virtual world. The parents can also ask for a guided tour of the smartphone and ask about the apps the child uses.

After the guided tour, parents should talk to the child about the different online risks (content, contact and commercial). This part of the talk can take place at another time, so as to allow the guided tour to finish on a positive note. However, the parents must set up a date with the child for this second part of the preparatory talk. Parents don't have to appear as experts, but rather should show awareness and concern. For every risk domain, they should ask the child whether he was exposed to any hazards, and how he dealt or would deal with them if they were to happen. Developing such scenarios creates parental presence. The parents should explain to the child the meaning and consequences of the risks involved in each domain. Preparing their questions in advance shows the child that they are serious about the matter. Far from being a disadvantage, this surplus formality actually increases the impact of the intervention. We propose the following list:

- "Did it ever happen to you that a stranger tried to contact you over the internet? Did anybody try to interest you in forbidden or dangerous activities?" "Did anyone try to interest you in gambling, drugs or sexual stories?" "Did anyone write or say anything that made you feel uncomfortable or ashamed?" "How would you react if any of those things were to happen?" "You can guess why we are asking you those questions. Many children have been tempted into dangerous meetings or activities over the internet. We want you to know that we'll always stand by you and help you protect yourself, or deal with a complicated situation. If something like that happens, please tell us. We promise not to be angry, but to do our best to help you!"

- "Did you buy things over the web, either with the computer or the smartphone?" "Did you download applications that cost money?" "Did you ever give our credit card number?" The parents then clarify: "It is important for you to be alert to those risks, because if you agree to any kind of proposition that costs money or requires a credit card, it may lead to trouble. Many children agree to a seemingly innocent offer, only to find out that they were tricked into a situation from which it was very difficult to get out." They may then add: "We want to make it clear that if we agree that you buy something with our credit card, our agreement refers only to that specific deal. In any case, we check all payments from our credit cards every month."
- "Did anybody offend you or slander you on Facebook or another social network?" "Did any such thing happen to any of your friends?" "Did you ever witness an attempt to ostracize someone on Facebook or another social network?" "How would you react to such an attempt?" After a pause the parents can add: "It is important that you know how to protect yourself and that you don't allow yourself to get involved in cyber-bullying. If anything like that happens to you, please tell us. We promise to do our best to help! And if you get in trouble, we'll do our best to support you and keep you from being shamed!"
- "Sometimes children tell things about themselves on their Facebook page or in blogs that afterwards they deeply regret. Did any of your friends make disclosures that might hurt them, now or in the future?" "If a friend makes disclosures that you think might hurt him, would you talk to him about it? Or do you think this would just be meddling and you shouldn't talk to him?" After a short pause, the parents may add: "It's important that you know, that disclosures that you make today may hurt you in the future. Kids disclose things about themselves to get sympathy, arouse curiosity or just get a response! Please don't do that, it may lead you into trouble!"
- "Were you ever exposed to pornography on the web?" If the child answers negatively, the parents may say: "If you still haven't been, you likely will be. If not on your own, then on your friends' computers or smartphones." "How would you react to an invitation to look at pornography with friends?" "Did you stumble on sites that invite you to gamble?" "Did you stumble on sites that glorify drugs or that praise all kinds of extreme diets?" "How will you react if you come across any of these?" After a short pause, the parents may add: "We're sure that you'll stumble on pornography on the web. It's just everywhere. We want you to know that pornography has nothing to do with positive sexuality. Pornography is full of lies. Those people do not really enjoy it; they only fake it. They do it only because of the money, or in exchange for drugs, or because they are forced to. We want you to know that pornography is a big lie!"

The last part of the talk should be devoted to a contract regarding safe use of the computer and smartphone. The parents can explain that a contract is signed when a special service is provided. The child has experience with applications that in order to be downloaded require the user to formally agree to the conditions of use. The same is true about the virtual services provided by the parents: their use should be contingent upon a signed commitment to use them safely. The parents, on their side, commit themselves to providing the child those services and doing their best to keep the child safe from trouble. In this way, the contract stipulates that exercising vigilant care is the parents' duty regarding the services they are providing. We propose the following text:

Parental commitment

- We commit ourselves to being available in case you require help with difficulties or dilemmas regarding the digital world.
- Our decisions regarding rules and limitations will take the importance of the internet in your life into consideration.
- We'll be vigilant about possible dangers, because it is our utmost duty as parents to care for your safety.
- We will not spy behind your back: all our activities will be carried out in the open.

Child's commitment

- I won't visit sites that are off-bounds for me. Specifically, I won't visit pornography or gambling sites or sites that propagate drugs or any kinds of damaging activities.
- I'll tell you immediately if anything happens that causes me offense or shame.
- I won't meet with strangers whom I met over the internet without your permission.
- I won't use the computer or smartphone in ways that may damage my sleep, my ability to function at school or in other scholastic activities. My virtual activities will not come at the expense of family activities, such as meals, family meetings or joint outings.
- I won't give information of an intimate nature about myself or my family. I'll consult with you if I have any doubts about the requested information.

The contract creates a commitment but is not, in itself, a guarantee that the child will honor its conditions. Far from obviating the need to continue exercising vigilant care, the contract actually helps legitimize it, justifying the parents' protective steps in case its conditions are not upheld. Moreover, if the child refuses to sign the contract, this is an alarm sign in itself, indicating that the child is probably using the computer or smartphone in inappropriate ways.

If the parents detect alarm signs indicating problematic use, they should take steps to protect the child from harm. The following are some typical danger signals: the child locks the door of his room when he is at the computer; sits at the computer until late at night; is active at night and sleeps in the daytime; orders commodities with the parents' credit card without permission; neglects scholastic, social and family activities; loses his interest in activities that are not linked to the computer; has outbursts when the parents "disturb" him at the computer; or refuses adamantly to answer the parents' questions regarding its use. When confronted with such signs, the parents should intensify their vigilant care. They should not act impulsively, nor expect that threats or punishments can solve the problem. However, if they take the time and effort to act patiently and decidedly, they will reduce the risks their child is exposed to.

When transitioning to higher levels of vigilant care, the parents should say so to the child openly. For instance:

> "We respect your privacy and your use of the internet, but some recent events have caused us serious concern. Therefore, we'll do all we can to understand the nature of your activities in the digital world and, if necessary, we'll act to limit your access."
>
> "We are aware of the importance the computer has in your life. But we see that lately, your use of the computer is detrimental to your sleep and your studies. Therefore, we'll do all we can to reduce the damage and guarantee that your use of the computer and smartphone is not harmful."

If the child tears up the written announcement or refuses to read it, the parents should answer in a quiet tone: "We didn't expect you to agree. We wrote you the announcement to be fair with you, so that things are not done behind your back. This announcement reflects our duty as parents!" After this answer, the parents should stop the discussion.

If the child sits at the computer till late at night, the parents should decide when it should be turned off. If the child does not abide by the stipulated time, the parents must take action to make that happen. However, under no circumstances should they push the power button off when the child is at the computer. Such an act often leads to severe escalation. Instead, the parents can tell the child that if he does not keep within the time limits, they will have to disconnect the computer. They should do this when the child is not at home, for instance by disconnecting the modem or the mouse. Another possible way is to tell the child: "You have five minutes to save and turn off the computer. After that time it will be our job to do so." If the child refuses, the parents can turn off the electricity in the whole house for a few seconds—this causes less escalation than pushing the computer's power button. It is helpful to have a supporter available (for instance, on the phone). The supporter can also tell the child beforehand that the parents are going to turn off the electricity if the child does not save and turn off the computer. The supporter should also tell the child that the parents' act is legitimate and reflects their care for his safety. If the parents believe the child will react violently, it is better to disconnect the computer only the next day, keeping it disconnected until the child renews his commitment to abide by the stipulated hours. Again, the help of a supporter can enhance their ability to do so. Supporters help in three major ways: by reducing escalation, by validating the parents' acts, and by the fact that a commitment that the child makes before a supporter is stronger than one made before the parents alone.

The parents can also stop providing internet services for a while. This is a serious step, which requires preparation. If the child uses the internet to download school materials as well, the parents have to find a solution for this problem as long as the internet is disconnected. Most parents are unaware that they can order internet services for specific hours of the day. This allows the parents to disconnect the internet during the night or in the morning, before the child goes to school. Parents should also know that trying to stipulate the number of hours the child can sit at the computer is usually unhelpful. This kind of parental rule leads to constant bickering and evasiveness. In contrast, deciding when the computer is to be turned off every night is much more feasible. It can be expected that a child who uses the computer around the clock will have difficulties adapting. Some children will feel cut off from their social world. This should not deter the parents. Our experience with dozens of families shows that most parents are capable of stopping the provision of harmful services, and that children gradually adapt to the new situation. Parents sometimes imagine the most terrible scenarios about what may happen. Those scenarios almost never materialize. Children resist, sometimes tenaciously, but if the parents are prepared and supported, they can withstand that. The result is that vigilant care is enhanced and the level of risk reduced.

In the previous chapters, we have described how parents can return to play a vital role in areas that had formerly been viewed as out of bounds for them. Thus, parents contacted the child's friends and talked to their parents, checked the child's room for drugs or stolen goods, and visited street corners. Some parents even contacted the purveyors of forbidden services, so as to show them that their child was not alone in the world. In all those cases, the parents dared to re-own their parenthood. Access to the virtual world is hindered by three different "locks": awe for the private sphere and for the world of technology, and fear of the child's reactions. However, with support, the great majority of parents can overcome their awe and fear and regain their parenthood in this troublesome area, as well.

Robert and Bea felt helpless when their daughter Rachel (16) stopped going to school, spent all her time on social networks and related to them with total disrespect. When the therapist proposed that they reduce Rachel's access to the internet, the father said: "That's extreme! It's as if you told me to cut off my daughter's hand or foot! How can I know this won't make her depressed or push her to attempt suicide?" In the course of the session, it turned out that Rachel had never threatened suicide and had no signs of depression. The therapist, however, made clear that even if there were suicide threats, the way to deal with them was not to free her from all limits and obligations. After their attempts to bring Rachel to a more moderate use failed, the parents disconnected the computer and stopped smartphone service. Rachel raved, but when she saw that the computer and the smartphone remained disconnected, she started to negotiate. The negotiations lasted for two weeks, during which the devices remained disconnected. This prolonged discussion period was due to the parents' decision that they had to see clear signs that Rachel was steadily back in school. When the devices were eventually reinstated, Rachel's total absorption did not recur. When, at the end of the treatment, the therapist reminded the parents of the father's metaphor about "cutting off his daughter's hand or foot," the father said: "It's hard to believe that I was so paralyzed!"

The Project

The interventions described above were incorporated into a three-session group treatment manual for parents. The manual was developed over a number of months, in the course of which 45 parents were treated and interviewed, and the interventions were gradually adapted to fit the parents' needs. The interviews allowed for a preliminary assessment of the training's acceptability. We call this kind of project "treatment development research," meaning research that helps develop a new treatment protocol (Zohar et al., submitted). This kind of preliminary study is seldom reported, as treatment manuals usually appear as if they were born ready-made, like Pallas Athena from the head of Zeus. This practice gives a false picture of treatment and research. The development of a detailed intervention is in itself the product of a careful investigation. What can be learned from treatment development research may be no less valuable than what we learn from randomized control trials. In effect, the conduct of such preparatory studies has been recommended as part of an optimal strategy for research in psychotherapy (Bruce & Sanderson, 2005). Unfortunately, the policy of most professional journals is almost exclusively to publish randomized controlled trials, while the process of development is left in the shadow. In our opinion, this is highly detrimental to the field of therapy.

In the present project, besides helping to tailor the intervention to the parents' needs and capacity, the preparatory study showed that parents felt they were making considerable gains. They showed good ability to transition between the levels of vigilant care; increased their parental knowledge regarding the child's activities in the digital world; succeeded in performing the basic steps, such as the preparatory talk and the involvement of supporters; and, in the few cases where this was required, also succeeded in taking unilateral steps to protect the child. In all cases, the parents' sense of legitimacy regarding their involvement in the child's digital world increased. In addition, the parents reported improvements in the child's functioning in the areas of school, family and social life (Geyra, 2011; Alexandron, 2012; Nataneli, 2013). In the wake of this preparatory work, we are now undertaking a randomized controlled trial. In this study, we hope to document the effectiveness of parental vigilant care not only on subjective, but also on objective measures of internet use, as we have already done in the case of young drivers (Shimshoni et al., 2013).

References

Alexandron, A. (2012). Computer overuse among children and adolescents. Unpublished master's thesis, School of Psychological Sciences, Tel-Aviv University.

Bruce, T. J. & Sanderson, W. C. (2005). Evidence-based psychosocial practices: Past, present and future. In Stout, C. E. & Hayes, R. A. (Eds.), *Evidence-based Practice: Methods, models and tools for mental health professionals* (pp. 220–243). Hoboken, NJ: John Wiley & Sons.

Cash, H., Rae, C. D., Steel, A. H. & Winkler, A. (2012). Internet addiction: A brief summary of research and practice. *Current Psychiatry Reviews*, *8*(4), 292.

De Moor, S., Dock, M., Gallez, S., Lenaerts, S., Scholler, C. & Vleugels, C. (2008). *Teens and ICT: Risks and opportunities*. Belgium: TIRO.

Geyra, A. (2011). Vigilant care and adolescent activities in the computer. Unpublished master's thesis, School of Psychological Sciences, Tel-Aviv University.

Kormas, G., Critselis, E., Janikian, M., Kafetzis, D. & Tsitsika, A. (2011). Risk factors and psychosocial characteristics of potential problematic and problematic internet use among adolescents: A cross-sectional study. *BMC Public Health*, *11*(1), 595.

Kowalski, R. M., Giumetti, G. W., Schroeder, A. N. & Lattanner, M. R. (2014). Bullying in the digital age: A critical review and meta-analysis of cyberbullying research among youth. *Psychological Bulletin*, *140*(4), 1073.

Livingstone, S. (2006). Drawing conclusions from new media research: Reflections and puzzles regarding children's experience of the Internet. *The Information Society*, *22*(4), 219–230.

Liu, T. C., Desai, R. A., Krishnan-Sarin, S., Cavallo, D. A. & Potenza, M. N. (2011). Problematic Internet use and health in adolescents: Data from a high school survey in Connecticut. *The Journal of Clinical Psychiatry*, *72*(6), 836.

Liu, Q.-X., Fang, X.-Y., Deng, L.-Y., & Zhang, J.-T. (2012). Parent–adolescent communication, parental Internet use and Internet-specific norms and pathological Internet use among Chinese adolescents. *Computers in Human Behavior*, *28*(4), 1269–1275.

Nataneli, O. (2013). Virtual parents: Parental presence in Facebook, Smartphone and some other new things. Unpublished master's thesis, School of Psychological Science, Tel-Aviv University.

Palfrey, J. & Gasser, U. (2013). *Born Digital: Understanding the first generation of digital natives*. New York: Basic Books.

Shapira, N. A., Lessig, M. C., Goldsmith, T. D., Szabo, S. T., Lazoritz, M., Gold, M. S. & Stein, D. J. (2003). Problematic internet use: Proposed classification and diagnostic criteria. *Depression and Anxiety*, *17*(4), 207–216.

Shimshoni, Y., Farah, H., Lotan, T., Grimberg, E., Dritter, O., Musicant, O. & Omer, H. (2013). Effects of parental vigilant care and feedback on novice driver risk. *Journal of Adolescence*, *38*, 69–80.

Wang, H., Zhou, X., Lu, C., Wu, J., Deng, X. & Hong, L. (2011). Problematic internet use in high school students in Guangdong province, China. PLoS One, *6*(5), e19660.

Williams, A. L. & Merten, M. J. (2011). iFamily: Internet and social media technology in the family context. *Family and Consumer Sciences Research Journal*, *40*(2), 150–170.

9 Diabetes[1]

with Yael Rothman-Kabir

Diabetes is one of the most prevalent chronic diseases in children, and its frequency is on the rise. Diabetic children must receive insulin from an external source by daily injections or via an insulin pump, so as to keep their glycemic levels balanced. Their nutrition must be strictly monitored, so that the appropriate insulin dosage may be calculated. Monitoring the child's sugar level continuously is crucial. Failing to follow this regimen may lead in the short term to hypo- or hyperglycemia, and in the long term to cardiovascular disease, micro-vascular damage, kidney damage, retinopathy, risk of organ amputation and death.

The nature of diabetes, as well as of other chronic illnesses, requires parents to be closely involved. In effect, with smaller children, a good glycemic balance is often achieved because the parents can control the daily monitoring of sugar levels and administration of insulin. However, during adolescence, adherence to the treatment regimen becomes more difficult, because of the child's growing autonomy and due to child–parent conflicts. Adolescents suffer considerably more from glycemic imbalance than children or adults. The adolescent's wish to be like others, and the desire to shake off parental control, aggravate these difficulties.

There are a number of reasons vigilant care is especially relevant for parents of diabetic adolescents: (a) It increases parental knowledge and presence. Studies show that these variables are linked to better adherence and glycemic balance (Berg et al., 2008). (b) It is structured in ways that reduce conflict and escalation (Lavi-Levavi, Shachar & Omer, 2013). Family conflict has been linked to poorer outcomes with diabetic adolescents (Jacobson et. al., 1994; Miller-Johnson et al., 1994). (c) It allows for an increase in autonomy in ways that are consonant with the adolescent's safety. This is crucial if we wish to foster not only better balance in the present, but also the development of self-care.

In order to train parents of diabetic adolescents in vigilant care, we developed a treatment protocol of ten individual sessions. The counselor first asks general questions regarding the house routine and problems in illness management. Thereupon, the counselor focuses on specific questions, such as: How many times does their child check her blood sugar every day? Does reminding help? Does the child take her diabetes equipment when she goes out? How do the parents respond if she refuses to do so? How informed are relatives, friends and school personnel regarding the illness and the demands of its care? The counselor then widens the attention to other areas, such as other behavior problems, level of parental knowledge, parent–child or parent–parent conflicts, and the parents' ability to get help and support.

The basic concepts of vigilant care are then introduced. Parents are often relieved when hearing that vigilant care is not an attempt to control the child, but to increase their parental presence. This presentation often signals a marked rise in their motivation already, in the very first session.

Parents are then coached on how to recognize and prevent escalation. They are helped to avoid nagging and arguing. Those processes are termed "ping-pong interactions," as they usually lead to unpleasant, repetitive and ineffective interchanges with the child. The parents are then trained on how to delay their reaction in case of conflict ("Strike when the iron is cold!") and to reduce controlling and domineering messages ("You don't have to win, only to persist!"). Such steps have proved effective in reducing escalation and parent–child conflicts (Lavi-Levavi, Shachar & Omer, 2013).

> Sam, a widower in our care, told the counselor that his son Jim (15) came back home at night, after having skipped his blood sugar measurements for a whole day. The moment he got home, the father asked him to measure his blood sugar immediately. Jim protested loudly, whereupon Sam threatened to ground him. The situation got worse when the father saw the result of the measurement. In the following week, the management of the diabetes and the father–son relationship became worse. In the next treatment session, the father was coached on how to manage similar situations in the future. He should quietly request his son check the blood sugar before going to sleep. If the boy refused, Sam would say: "I request you do that now, because your sugar level is probably high, and we have to do something about it. I won't make a scene upon seeing the results, but only take the necessary steps to guarantee your sugar balance. We'll discuss this tomorrow, because we're both too upset to have a good conversation now!" Sam role-played with the counselor how the conversation could be conducted without threats or ping-pong interactions. The following day, if his son was still uncooperative, Sam would involve a supporter.

An important treatment task is the establishment of a better family routine. A clear and stable structure helps the parents anchor themselves and stabilize the child. The goals of the routine are: (a) To help parents exercise vigilant care over illness-related behaviors. Thus, one of the recommended rules is that eating is henceforth to be conducted at the dinner table. The parents are specifically coached on how to resist problematic habits, like eating in front of the television or in the child's room. (b) To help parents change problematic family habits. For example, eliminating sugary soft drinks from the house. (c) To prevent escalation: A clear routine reduces the sense that parental decisions are arbitrary, thus reducing arguments. (d) To create an environment that is as similar as possible to that of all family members. Thus, the child with diabetes is no longer the only one who has to eat at the table. His siblings are now also required to do so. A home routine thus helps the child with diabetes feel less different and isolated.

> Jenny's (14) mother, Alice, used to have a stock of sweets locked up in a drawer. Alice herself had a sweet tooth, so this was a way of keeping sweets in the house in a way that made them less available for her diabetic daughter. The result, however, was that Jenny got into constant fights with her, often succeeding in getting her mother to unlock the drawer with the sweets. For this family, the rule that there would be no sweets in the house was a modest but important start.

The parents' active resistance to harmful illness behaviors begins with a formal announcement, delivered to the child both verbally and in writing. The announcement opens with the parents' commitment to doing everything in their power to combat the illness. They then detail two or three negative behaviors that they will resist. They declare that they will no longer keep the situation at home a secret, but will get help from whoever is willing to support them. The announcement ends with an expression of love and commitment. Parents plan separate announcements to the diabetic child and her siblings. This is necessary, because siblings are also affected by the changes in the home routine, and are expected to carry it out. The counselor helps the parents cope with possible negative reactions to the announcement. Preparing the announcement is also a good way to help the parents deal with their own reservations regarding the need to impose limits that affect all members of the family.

The role of supporters is highly significant in families with a diabetic child. Their backing and legitimation can help the family withstand the challenges of the treatment regime. Nevertheless, many parents are reluctant to involve supporters, objecting that their burden cannot be shared with others, that their child will suffer shame or that others are too busy with their own problems to be able to help. Parents find it especially difficult to disclose to relatives and friends the fact that the diabetic child sometimes displays extreme behaviors in order to rebuff parental demands. Convincing the parents to give up their objections and ask others for help requires tact, patience and empathy. In our experience, the ability to do so is the mark of a more experienced counselor. The supporters can help in a number of ways, such as: telling the child they are aware he is not cooperating; reinforcing parental messages; talking with the child about his difficulties, and helping develop possible solutions; taking care that when the child is with them he monitors his blood level and acts accordingly; and mediating between child and parents to achieve reasonable agreements.

Three special tools in vigilant care in diabetes are: planned text messages, "diabetes talks" and reminders. Planned text messages are used when the child is away or on days when there are no family meals. The child is then requested to send a short text message at an agreed time, telling the parents about the sugar measurement. Parents are trained on how to deal with the child's possible resistance to this procedure, while avoiding escalation.

Diabetes talks focus on the last sugar measurements and recent management issues. The frequency of the talks depends on the required level of vigilant care. Thus, if the parents have to act at the highest level (protective steps), diabetes' talks are to be held every evening. The frequency is lowered if warning signs diminish. Initially, both parents should be present; subsequently, only one. In the meeting, the parents review with the child what happened in the last day or days (sugar measurements, difficult points, failures and successes). Parents are coached on how to avoid clashes and ping-pong interactions. The goal of these talks is to manifest presence, learn from mistakes and convey the message that the child is not alone in his struggle. The child should be encouraged for any improvements, however small. This should be done in an appreciative tone, without preaching. Thus, it is not a good idea to say: "You see, when you want you can take good care of yourself! So why don't you do so always?" A rebellious child may take this as a cue to show her parents that she'll have her way. Instead, the parents' messages should convey a sense of togetherness and respect. If the parents maintain their self-control and avoid rebuking the child, searching instead for constructive solutions for the difficulties, the talk will likely have positive effects. If the child does not cooperate, or answers provocatively, the parents can say: "We don't accept this! We'll weigh our steps and tell you what we've decided!" For instance, the parents may decide that in the coming week sugar levels will be measured in the presence of one of the parents or a supporter.

Reminders are a complex issue in the management of diabetes, among other reasons because the child has to perform many acts related to the illness on a daily basis. Parents who try to remind the child all the time will quickly become exhausted. Besides, many children habituate to the parents' reminders, turning them into "background noise." Therefore, it is important to reach an agreement with the child about acceptable ways to remind him. The following are some kinds of reminders that proved helpful with different families: the use of short written messages that are placed on the child's plate or with her sandwich, a daily text message (many of these are messages of appreciation) or having supporters send reminders to the child. If the parents manage reminders wisely and avoid overwhelming the child with a flood of messages, their presence in the child's mind will be positively enhanced.

A special session in the treatment is devoted to helping the parents bring out "the child's voice" in an empathic manner. Helping the parents give empathic expression to the child's experience helps them feel that the treatment is not inflicted upon the child, but takes her suffering to heart. The parents are helped to put into words the difficulties the child undergoes in developing a positive identity in the face of her illness, in dealing with the hardships of the regimen and in finding her place among peers. At the end of this session, the parents draft a message of support that empathically acknowledges the child's difficulties, while stressing their own commitment to stand by her.

"Dear Maggy,

We know we demand a lot from you. We see how hard it is for you to live under a regimen of blood tests, insulin injections and dietary restrictions. We understand what it means to wish to be free, like all other kids, and yet to feel different. We identify with you and admire your strength. We want you to know that we think often about how you're feeling. We'll stand by your side and fight together with you against the illness. We want you to know we are here for you! Love, Mom and Dad".

The Project[2]

The first stage in the project was devoted to the development of the treatment protocol. An initial version was written and tried out with a number of families. The parents were interviewed at the end of the treatment, and their reactions were used to improve the intervention. A number of discussions with the counselors who conducted the treatments led to the final version. The second, ongoing stage is an outcome study conducted in parallel in four treatment centers.[3] The study follows a within-subject design with repeated measures. The families are measured before and after a waiting period of 10 weeks, after 10 weeks of treatment and at follow-up after 10 additional weeks. Both parents and child are given questionnaires to fill. Data are also retrieved from the glucometer, indicating the number and results of blood sugar measurements.

The chief variables in the study are: family conflict around the illness; parental vigilant care; parental helplessness; parental anchoring; child motivation and diabetes management skills; and diabetes self-care.[4] Glucometer and metabolic data provide the objective measures in the study.

At this point, we are able to summarize our preliminary results from the first 23 families participating in the study. These results are based on the three first measurements of the self-report tools. The glucometer and metabolic results have not yet been analyzed. The results up to now confirm our clinical impression: Parents report a decline in family conflict, improved vigilant care and better management of the diabetes. The child's report shows improved self-care, thus confirming the parents' reports. Parents who concluded the treatment said that the approach is changing their ability to cope with the illness in far-reaching ways. A single mother of a diabetic boy told us:

"I thought that I was on top of things, and that everything was okay the way I handled things before. But the truth is that the diabetes was out of control. I didn't have any say at home about adherence to the regimen. I only threatened and felt helpless. Now things are very different. I understood there were changes I had to make at home, and made them. Today was the first time that my son was not afraid to come to the clinic visit. He was proud of himself and of his sugar levels. And so was I."

Notes

1 Although this chapter is about diabetes, it is potentially relevant for other chronic illnesses as well.
2 This study was supported by the Otzma Foundation and JDRF, Israel.
3 The Endocrinology unit in Safra Children's Hospital, Sheba Medical Center; Maccabi Health Care diabetes clinic, Ra'anana; Children's Endocrinology unit, Assaf Haroffe Medical Center, Ramla; and Children's Endocrinology unit, Sha'arey Tzedek Hospital, Jerusalem.
4 Details on the specific questionnaires can be had on request from Yael Rothman-Kabir, yael_rk@hotmail.com.

References

Berg, C. A., Butler, J. M., Osborn, P., King, G., Palmer, D. L., Butner, J. and Wiebe, D. J. (2008). Role of parental monitoring in understanding the benefits of parental acceptance on adolescent adherence and metabolic control of type 1 diabetes. *Diabetes Care*, *31*(4), 678–683.

Jacobson, A. M., Hauser, S. T., Lavori, P., Willett, J. B., Cole, C. F., Wolfsdorf, J. I. and Wertlieb, D. (1994). Family environment and glycemic control: A four-year prospective study of children and adolescents with insulin-dependent diabetes mellitus. *Psychosomatic Medicine*, *56*(5), 401–409.

Lavi-Levavi, I., Shachar, I. & Omer, H. (2013). Training in nonviolent resistance for parents of violent children: Differences between fathers and mothers. *Journal of Systemic Therapies*, *32*(4), 79–93.

Miller-Johnson, S., Emery, R. E., Marvin, R. S., Clarke, W. et al. (1994). Parent–child relationships and the management of insulin-dependent diabetes mellitus. *Journal of Consulting and Clinical Psychology*, *62*(3), 603–610.

10 Vigilant Care Among Juvenile Offenders

Haim Omer and Zohar Lotringer in collaboration with the Israeli Juvenile Probation Service[1] and the Or Yarok Association for Prevention of Road Accidents

The age range for juvenile offenders[2] in most countries is from 12 to 18 (Agnew, 2005; Annual statistical abstract by the Israel National Council for the Child, 2015). In the US, juvenile offenders are responsible for approximately 11% of all criminal offenses (Federal Bureau of Investigation, 2013). Recent data released by the Office of Juvenile Justice and Delinquency Prevention (OJJDP) indicate that there are approximately 1.7 million juvenile court cases in a given year in the United States (Knoll & Sickmund, 2010; Puzzanchera, Adams & Sickmund, 2010). The situation in many other countries is probably similar.

Therapeutic interventions for offending youth have been intensely researched (Sawyer, Borduin & Dopp, 2015; Schwalbe, Gearing, MacKenzie, Brewer & Ibrahim, 2012). Interventions that are focused on the adolescent include individual (Arthur & Reppucci, 1993; Kazdin, 1992; Kazdin, Bass, Siegel & Thomas, 1989) and group therapy (Cecile & Born, 2009; Lipsey, Wilson & Cothern, 2000; Nas, Brugman & Koops, 2005). Although both modalities have shown some positive effects, some studies indicate that group therapy for juvenile offenders may have negative consequences, due to the potential harmful influences of associating with other juvenile offenders (Bayer, Pintoff & Pozen, 2004; Cecile & Born, 2009; Sawyer, Borduin & Dopp, 2015). In addition, focusing on the adolescent is probably not as efficient as working with parents or other caretakers as well (National Institute for Health and Care Excellence, 2013). Many studies show family therapy and parental training to be effective in reducing delinquent and antisocial behaviors, as well as improving the child's and the parents' functioning and well-being (Armstrong, Wilks, McEvoy, Russel & Melivelle, 1994; Bank, Marlowe, Reid, Patterson & Weinrott, 1991; Schwalbe, Gearing, MacKenzie, Brewer & Ibrahim, 2012; Scott, Sylva, Doolan, Price, Jacobs, Crook & Landau, 2010).

Due to the difficulty of treating juvenile offenders, most of these treatments include highly intensive and often prolonged interventions, which make them difficult to apply on a broad basis (Armstrong, Wilks, McEvoy, Russel & Melivelle, 1994; Kazdin, 1992; Miller, 2014; Welsh & Greenwood, 2014). In addition, parental drop-out rates are high, often reaching up to 50% of the participants (Arthur & Reppucci, 1993; Hawkins, Catalano, Jones & Fine, 1987).

The fact that vigilant care is an appealing concept for parents, that training can be relatively short and that the literature shows its relevance for many risk conditions (see Chapter 1) makes the development of a short-term group training for parents of juvenile offenders a promising endeavor. Such an intervention would aim at training the parents on how to exercise vigilant care at the appropriate levels, increase parental presence and knowledge, create support and legitimacy and reduce escalation and conflict.

The Project

The first stage of the project was dedicated to the development of a treatment manual[3] and a preliminary examination of the intervention's acceptability and relevance for the parents. A provisional intervention was formulated and tested with two groups (with 10 and 8 parents). The intervention included 12 weekly sessions, and one follow-up meeting two months afterwards. Between sessions, the trainers (juvenile probation officers) maintained contact with the parents via phone calls and text messages, reminding them of the main points of the previous session and encouraging them to complete the home assignments. Recruiting parents of juvenile offenders to participate in therapeutic programs is a known challenge. Therefore, special attention was devoted to this issue. The trainers were coached on specific ways to address the parents' reservations and arouse their interest, paying special attention to the recruitment of fathers, who are usually less motivated to attend.

Training begins with a discussion of the principles of vigilant care. The importance of parental presence, knowledge and self-control are highlighted and illustrated. Parents are helped to understand that their goal is not to control the child, but to increase parental knowledge, involvement and presence in the child's life. Special emphasis is placed on preventing escalation. The parents are coached on how to prepare in advance for the child's reactions, improve their self-control, delay their responses ("Strike when the iron is cold!") and show persistence in their vigilant care ("You don't have to win, but only to persist!").

The parents are then coached on how to write and deliver an announcement, in which they state their decision to resist the child's negative behaviors, such as curfew violations or lying about his whereabouts and activities. Delivery of the announcement is role-played in the session, and the parents develop specific coping strategies for the child's possible reactions to the announcement.

The parents are then trained in the various levels of vigilant care. The *traffic light metaphor* helps them identify and evaluate warning signals. *Green light* refers to situations that allow the parents to stay at the level of open attention; *yellow light* to signs that require a transition to focused attention; and *red light* to situations requiring actual protective steps. The metaphor helps the parents perform quick assessments, enabling them to match their attitude to the child's behavior. Parents reported that this tool helped them react without the usual hesitation and sense of paralysis that characterized them in the past. The parents learn that open attention never stops, even when they undertake actions pertaining to the levels of focused attention and protective steps. They are coached on how to develop and demonstrate interest and involvement in the teenager's life, increase non-invasive contacts with him[4] and with people in his surroundings and initiate conversations regarding specific risk factors. Guidelines are provided on how to make the transition to focused attention, question the child and establish clear rules. Special attention is given to the parental steps pertaining to the uppermost level of vigilant care, like the telephone round and parental visitations to street corners or friends' houses in which the child is staying without permission. Parental coping with the child's possible reactions is discussed and role-played. Practice assignments are given at the end of each session.

Two sessions are devoted to the development of a support network. Parents learn how the support network can serve as *a safety net* that protects the child from crashing in difficult situations, *an alarm system* with multiple sensors that helps detect danger signs, and *a source of legitimacy* that validates parental vigilant care. Though involvement of relatives and family friends has been linked to lower risk (e.g., Dornbusch et al., 1985), the parents of juvenile offenders often find it difficult to ask for support, among other reasons, out of shame and guilt. Those difficulties are specifically addressed in the training. Parents discuss and role-play how to address potential supporters and present them their plight. Though some of the parents succeeded in overcoming the hurdle and asking their relatives and friends for help, others found it difficult to reach out. This was partly compensated for by the support parents received from other group participants. We hope the changes we made in the treatment protocol in the wake of our preliminary results will improve their ability to contact supporters.

A preliminary evaluation was conducted, in which the parents who received training in vigilant care were compared to "treatment as usual" (TAU) as administered by the Israel Juvenile Probation Service (TAU consisted of regular meetings with the teenagers and a couple of supportive sessions for the parents). The parents were assessed at three time points (before treatment, after treatment and at a two months' follow-up). The findings showed that the training is well accepted, practicable and seen as very helpful by the parents. The parents in the vigilant care groups reported a decrease in parental helplessness and an increase in parental anchoring and knowledge (Lotringer et al., submitted[5]). The parents reported that the intervention equipped them with practical tools, and that they experienced substantial improvement in well-being, self-control and sense of efficacy, as well as in communication with their child. An important finding regards the dropout level, as none of the participants in the vigilant care groups dropped out, reflecting the training's high appeal. Parental comments were nothing less than enthusiastic. In the words of one mother:

> "I have undergone a revolution in the way I handle things… I've participated in many parenting workshops before, but in this one things changed in my mind and I started to implement… I am so happy to have been a part of this group! It was such a difficult time for us, meeting the police and all… and now I think that maybe everything happened for the best, since we have woken up and otherwise we wouldn't have been here and learned so many things…."

The encouraging results of the pilot led to the second, controlled stage of our project, in which 120 parents of offending juveniles undergoing vigilant care parent training are being systematically compared to TAU. Parental variables include parenting functioning, self-efficacy, knowledge, ability to recognize warning signs and transition between the levels of vigilant care. In addition, evaluations by the probation officers, as well as recidivism after one year, may give an indication of the intervention's impact on the juveniles' risk levels. We are now halfway through the project, and the results of the pilot are being confirmed.

Notes

1. The Juvenile Probation Service (JPS) in Israel is under the jurisdiction of the Ministry of Social Affairs. It is responsible for treating minors aged 12–18 who are suspected or accused of a criminal act. The JPS applies a social-therapeutic working model; therefore, all probation officers are social workers.
2. The term "juvenile offenders" is the term used by the Israeli JPS, as it is considered to be less stigmatic than "juvenile delinquents."
3. The treatment manual was written by Z. Lotringer, Y. Everett (Tel-Aviv University), V. Rappaport, D. Nitzan, O. Eldar, O. Farash, R. Arazi-Shiff (Juvenile Probation Service), E. Grimberg, S. Tal (the Or Yarok Association) & H. Omer. The manual has been translated into English and is available upon request.
4. The present project was conducted with boys. However, we believe the manual is equally relevant for girls.
5. The questionnaires and the article describing the pilot are available upon request.

References

Agnew, R. (2005). *Juvenile Delinquency: Causes and control* (second ed.). Los Angeles: Roxbury Publishing Company.

Armstrong, H., Wilks, C., McEvoy, L., Russel, M. & Melivelle, C. (1994) Group therapy for parents of youth with a conduct disorder. *CMAJ*, *151*(7), 939–944.

Arthur, W. M. & Reppucci, N. D. (1993). The prevention and treatment of juvenile delinquency: A review of the research. *Clinical Psychology Review*, *13*, 133–167.

Bank, L., Marlowe, H., Reid, B. J., Patterson, R. G. & Weinrott, R. M. (1991). A comparative evaluation of parent-training interventions for families of chronic delinquents. *Journal of Abnormal Psychology*, *19*(1), 15–33.

Bayer, P., Pintoff, R. & Pozen, D. (2004). Building criminal capital behind bars: Peer effects in juvenile corrections (paper no. 864). New Haven, CT: Yale University, Economic Growth Center discussion.

Cecile, M. & Born M. (2009). Interventions in juvenile delinquency: Danger or iatrogenic effects? *Children and Youth Service Review*, *31*, 1217–1221.

Dornbusch, S., Carlsmith, J., Bushwall, S., Ritter, P., Leiderman, H., Hastorf, A. & Gross, R. (1985). Single parents, extended households, and the control of adolescents. *Child Development*, *56*, 326–341.

Federal Bureau of Investigation (2013). *Crime in the United States, 2012*. Washington, DC: U.S. Department of Justice.

Hawkins, J. D., Catalano, R. F, Jones, G. & Fine, D. (1987). Delinquency prevention through parent training: Results and issues from work in progress. In J. Q. Wilson & G. C. Loury (Eds.), *From Children to Citizens: Families, schools, and delinquency prevention*, *3*, 186–204.

Kazdin, A. E. (1992), Cognitive problem-solving skills training and parent management training in the treatment of antisocial behavior in children. *Journal of Consulting and Clinical Psychology*, *60*(5), 733–747.

Kazdin, A. E., Bass, D., Siegel, X. & Thomas, C. (1989). Cognitive-behavioral therapy and relationship therapy in the treatment of children referred for antisocial behavior. *Journal of Consulting and Clinical Psychology*, *57*, 522–535.

Knoll, C. & Sickmund, M. (2010). Delinquency cases in juvenile court, 2007 (OJJDP Fact Sheet). Washington, DC: Office of Juvenile Justice & Delinquency Prevention, Office of Justice Programs, U.S. Department of Justice.

Lipsey, M. W., Wilson, D. B. & Cothern, L. (2000). Effective intervention for serious offenders. Washington, DC: Department of Justice, Office of Juvenile Justice and Delinquency Prevention.

Miller, L. (2014). Juvenile crime and juvenile justice: Patterns, models, and implications for clinical and legal practice. *Aggression and Violent Behavior*, *19*, 122–137.

Nas, C., Brugman, D. & Koops, W. (2005). Effects of a multicomponent peer intervention program for juvenile delinquents on moral judgment, cognitive distortions, social skills and recidivism. *Psychology, Crime, & Law*, *11*, 421–434.

National Institute for Health and Care Excellence (2013). Antisocial behaviour and conduct disorders in children and young people: Recognition, intervention and management. NICE clinical guideline 158, www.guidance.nice.org.uk/cg158.

Puzzanchera, C., Adams, B. & Sickmund, M. (2010). Juvenile court statistics 2006–2007. Pittsburgh, PA: National Center for Juvenile Justice.

Sawyer, M. S., Borduin, M. C. & Dopp, A. R. (2015). Long-term effects of prevention and treatment on youth antisocial behavior: A meta-analysis. *Clinical Psychotherapy Review*, http://dx.doi.org/10.1016/j.cpr.2015.06.009.

Schwalbe, S. C., Gearing, E. R., MacKenzie, J. M., Brewer. B. K. & Ibrahim, R. (2012). A meta-analysis of experimental studies of diversion programs for juvenile offenders. *Clinical Psychology Review*, *32*, 26–33.

Scott, S., Sylva, K., Doolan, M., Price. J., Jacobs, B., Crook, C. & Landau, S. (2010). Randomised controlled trial of parent groups for child antisocial behavior targeting multiple risk factors: The SPOKES project. *Child Psychology and Psychiatry*, *51*, 48–57.

The Israel National Council for the Child (2015). *The State of the Child in Israel*. Jerusalem: Haruv Institute (published in Hebrew).

Welsh, B. C. & Greenwood, P. W. (2014). Making it happen: State progress in implementing evidence-based programs for delinquent youth. *Youth Violence and Juvenile Justice*, *13*(3), 243–257.

11 Teen Driving

with C. T. Juravel and Y. Shimshoni

Car accidents are the major cause of death among teens and young adults (Patton et al., 2009; Williams, 2003). The majority of severe accidents in this age group are caused by male drivers. The first year of driving and the first three months of independent driving, in particular, are the most dangerous (Simons-Morton et al., 2011; Lotan & Toledo, 2007). A number of factors have been implicated in those risks (Williams, Tefft & Grabowski, 2012):

- Young drivers do not have the experience to discern situations requiring higher alertness.
- Young drivers are prone to more aggressive driving.
- Young drivers have high susceptibility to peer influence.
- Young drivers endanger themselves particularly during weekends. The high risk is then probably due to the free atmosphere of those outings, and the possible influence of alcohol or other substances.

Those factors may be relevant for the majority of male teen drivers. It is probably a mistake for parents to think that their son is immune to those dangers.

In order to deal with this problem, many countries have modified the process of licensing, adding a period where the new driver is required to be accompanied by an experienced one (Williams, Tefft & Grabowski, 2012). Research has shown that throughout the accompanied-driving period, the involvement of young drivers in car accidents is very low, even when compared to experienced drivers (Glendon, 2014). However, when this period comes to an end, crash rates rise dramatically (Simons-Morton et al., 2011; Lotan & Toledo, 2007). This is a clear indication of how parental presence may affect teen driving. The question is whether parental presence could be effective over and beyond the period of accompanied driving, particularly if manifested in less direct ways, such as through vigilant care. In what follows, we illustrate how training in vigilant care can help parents become present in the mind of the new driver in ways that may considerably reduce risk.

The Accompanied-Driving Period

It is very important to allow the young driver to drive as much as possible during this period. For instance, he[1] can be allowed to be the driver on every family outing. It is also important to help him gain experience under different driving conditions, such as nighttime, heavy traffic and rain.

Accompanied driving has its own difficulties. The young driver often feels he knows how to drive, while the parents are highly sensitive to his shortcomings (Williams, Tefft & Grabowski, 2012). This situation may lead to arguments that turn each drive into a potential ordeal. As a result, many parents prefer to avoid the sessions of accompanied driving, waiting passively for the required period to end. How can these difficulties be overcome? It helps if the accompanying parent learns to postpone her remarks, making them only after the drive is over. This illustrates the principle of delay ("Strike when the iron is cold!"), which has been shown to reduce parent–child conflicts in different areas (Lavi-Levavi, Shachar & Omer, 2013; Weinblatt & Omer, 2008). The principle of delay is explained also to the teen driver, thus allowing him to participate in its implementation. In the words of one of the young drivers that we interviewed: "If we are driving together and my mother makes a remark, I tell her not to pressure me during the drive, and she accepts that." It is important that the accompanying parent choose no more than two points to comment upon. A higher quantity of remarks would cause cognitive and emotional overload, thus making it difficult for the young driver to profit from them. The young driver's readiness to accept parental remarks grows if the parents encourages him to comment on their own driving, as well. For instance: "During the accompanied drives I comment on your driving. I'll be glad if you comment on my driving too. I promise to take your remarks seriously!" By taking the child into consideration when they are driving, the parents make it more likely that he will keep them in mind when he is driving. One of the young drivers stated: "I like the fact that I can comment on their driving. I pay more attention to it, and my parents accept it. It also helped that they comment on my driving only after we finish driving, which is far less stressful." It is important that the parents stand by their commitment to take the young driver's comments seriously. If the parent says: "I can do that, because I'm more experienced!" the results will probably be negative. However, if the parent makes a serious attempt to improve his own driving in the wake of his child's comments, the young driver will probably drive more carefully, as well. This is particularly meaningful when the parent tends to drive aggressively. The parent can say candidly: "I want to participate in your effort to develop safe driving skills. I'll do my best to drive more carefully, so as to be with you in that!"

Parents are advised to institute "drivers' talks," where all family members comment on their driving experiences. Challenging situations and observations about other drivers are brought up and discussed. By encouraging the young driver to take active part in those conversations, he becomes incorporated into "the family of drivers."

The Transition to "Solo" Driving

The transition to driving on one's own may be one of those points in life that justify a rite of passage. Giving the keys to the young driver expresses the parents' trust and the fact that they now see their child as mature enough to drive on his own. However, given the importance and the potential risk involved in this transition, it would be advisable to emphasize it in a more formal way than it is usually done—for instance, by means of a preparatory talk and the signing of an agreement.[2] When parents entrust their child with a new and potentially dangerous tool, signing an agreement is justified. After all, the child has experienced having to sign an agreement, for instance, when getting a new application for the smartphone. The agreement would then signify that use of the car is conditional on the child's abiding by the safety rules.

The purpose of the proposed "transition rite" is to increase parental presence in the mind of the young driver. Signing the agreement adds legitimacy to further acts of vigilant care. As one of the parents put it: "It helps both sides: He knows his limitations, and I know that I have a toolbox." The parents can say: "The fact that we are giving you the keys to the car shows that we trust you. But we all know that the first year of driving is dangerous, and most of the accidents happen during this period. In order for all of us to stay safe and calm, we ask that you sign this agreement and commit yourself to safe driving." The parents are coached to make two additional requests: (a) That the young driver send them two short text messages whenever he goes out for the day or the evening, the first upon arrival at his destination, the second before midnight. (b) That whenever he drives to a new or distant destination, the young driver sits with one of the parents for a few minutes to prepare for the ride. This discussion should include:

- *The drive's destination*: Knowing the destination increases parental presence in the young driver's mind.
- *The course of the drive*: The inexperienced driver has to pay attention to many different things at once. Planning the route in advance simplifies the process of decision-making, reducing the driver's cognitive load. One young driver in the project said: "The fact that we think beforehand about the course of the drive gives me more confidence."
- *Distractions*: Parents can mention potential distractions that increase risk. One of the chief potential distractors is the cell phone (Williams, Tefft & Grabowski, 2012). Parents should ask the child specifically to turn off the cell phone before he leaves.
- *Additional passengers*: Research shows that risk grows with each additional passenger (Curry, Mirman, Kallan, Winston & Durbin, 2012). We recommend that for the first three months of independent driving, the limit should be one passenger. This could be a good place to raise the subject of peer pressure upon driving, and how the young driver would react in such a situation.

- *Time and conditions of return*: The young driver should tell the parent the intended time of return. If for any reason there is a delay of more than half an hour, the young driver should inform his parents. If the youngster drinks, he should agree to return by taxi, or ask the parents to pick him up, even if this is uncomfortable for both sides.

The very fact that this discussion takes place helps strengthen parental presence in the child's mind and helps reduce the risk, even if the young driver does not keep all his commitments.

As mentioned, when the young driver goes out at night, he should send two text messages: upon arriving at his destination and before midnight. The messages can be short ("I've arrived" and "Good night"). The very fact of having to send the messages keeps the parents in his mind. One young driver commented on the messages and the route planning: "It gave me a feeling that even if there's nobody with me in the car, it was like there was someone with me… you understand, in the beginning I felt anxious driving alone. So this helped me to be less anxious, it was like someone was with me." We could hardly imagine a more cogent testimony to the impact of vigilant care.

Here are some typical warning signals that justify intensifying vigilant care:

- Failure to comply with the agreed conditions. For instance, refusing to send text messages or coming later than agreed without informing the parent.
- Signs of dangerous driving, for instance, getting a ticket for speeding.
- Accidents—even very small accidents—can justify a temporary return to accompanied driving. A short period of accompanied driving can help understand what led to the accident and how this can be prevented in the future.

Some parents feel uncomfortable about these requirements, thinking them invasive of the young driver's privacy. This is a typical example of the lack of legitimacy parents often feel in exercising vigilant care. Actually, those requests are very modest. Parents who give their children the car should be allowed to sleep soundly, rather than staying awake in anxious expectation. Therefore, when the young driver objects to their requests, they should tell him squarely: "Look, I'm giving you the keys of the car! What am I asking in exchange? That you send me two text messages! That's a very small request indeed!" or "I don't want to call your friends, but I'll do so if you don't inform me when you're delayed. After all, I have the right to sleep calmly!" Parents who still feel apprehensive on account of the privacy reflex should be reminded that driving is no private matter, but an activity in a public space that concerns all other drivers and pedestrians. There is possibly no area of life where considerations of privacy are less relevant. Parents should say this clearly to the young driver. The youngster may of course disagree, but vigilant care does not depend on his consent. The parents can explain to the young driver the rationale behind their stance, but the young driver's agreement is not a condition for vigilant care. The parents can add to the legitimacy of their requests by asking a supporter to tell the young driver that though she respects his privacy, driving is not a private matter and that the parents are fully justified in their demands. In our project, the great majority of young drivers cooperated with the parents' requests, and only in a few cases was the involvement of supporters required.

Limiting Driving Rights

When warning signals multiply, and the young driver refuses to keep his side of the agreement, the parents may have to take protective steps and limit his driving rights, particularly in situations of higher risk, such as driving at night and on weekends. Parents who decide to protect their child can maintain their decision in spite of his protests. In such cases, they can apply the principles we described in Chapter 3 on how to implement vigilant care when the child resists. The parents should keep in mind that giving in to the pressure of a young driver who probably drives irresponsibly is tantamount to relinquishing his safety.

> Will and Vivian asked for help with their son Joe (17) in the wake of difficulties during the accompanied-driving period. Joe complained that his mother criticized him all the time. Vivian agreed she was anxious and worried. Will, however, backed his wife, saying that Joe had to restrain his impulsive driving. During the last weeks of accompanied driving, Vivian promised Joe to keep her remarks to a minimum and to voice them only after the drive was over. Joe answered provocatively: "You know you can't do that!" Vivian responded with humor: "At least it won't be only you who will have to control yourself in driving. I'll have to control my mouth too!" This proved to be a good opening and the last weeks of accompanied driving were conflict free. Joe then signed an agreement with his parents, but only partially kept his side. The parents, however, chose not to confront him at that stage. However, one month after he started driving solo, Joe scraped the car when backing out carelessly. The next day, Will told him: "You say we don't trust you. That's not true; we always let you drive on our family drives, even when your sister's baby is with us in the car. There's no bigger trust than that. But it is clear that when you're on your own, you drive carelessly. We'll now go out for a ride, and if everything is OK, you'll get all your driving rights back. But you'll have to abide by the agreement fully and send text messages as agreed." From then on, Joe abided by his commitment. Two weeks after his accident, he called his parents in the middle of the night, and said he had been drinking and was afraid to drive back. To his surprise, both

his parents came to fetch him. Joe rode back in the passenger's seat with Vivian, and Will returned in his own car. Vivian did not say a word during the drive back, but the next day, she told Joe that though at first she and Will were angered by the late call, on second thought they concluded he had acted correctly. The atmosphere improved, and so did Joe's driving, as shown by the data collected in the study.

The Project

In the first stage of the project,[3] a detailed protocol was developed to train parents of young drivers, after licensure but before the start of solo driving. The training lasted 90 minutes and was conducted in the family home. The young driver was present during the training, and an attempt was made to gain his cooperation by stressing that by showing he was responsible he would quickly earn full status as a driver. The trainer stressed that the young driver should have the opportunity to drive as much as possible, if he abided by the rules.

The development of the training protocol was followed by an objective evaluation of driving risk (Shimshoni et al., 2015). An IVDR (in-vehicle data recorder) appliance, which records events of excessive maneuvers, was installed in the family's car. Five driving elements were assessed: braking, accelerating, turn handling, lane handling and speeding. The system provides the young drivers and their parents with feedback on driving risk level. The families that participated in the experiment were randomly divided into four groups.

- *Control group*: None of the drivers in this group received any feedback or training.
- *Individual feedback, no training*: In this group, each family member received feedback on his own driving, but not on that of other family members. Thus, parents did not have access to the driving records of their teens, and vice versa. The parents in this group did not receive training in vigilant care.
- *Family feedback, no training*: In this group, family members were exposed to their own driving records and to those of other family members. Thus, parents had access to the driving records of the teen, and vice versa. The parents in this group did not receive training in vigilant care.
- *Family feedback plus parental training*: Family members had access to the driving data of all other family members as in the previous group. In addition, parents received 90 minutes' training in vigilant care.

Results showed that training in vigilant care reduced driving risk significantly. The gains were maintained for the six months of the study, thus showing that the effects of the training endured. The gains were particularly significant for young drivers who, early in the accompanied-driving period, had shown higher aggressive-driving tendencies. An interview with a sample of parents and young drivers showed that parents were both willing and able to implement the required steps. Of special importance is the fact that parental interventions were well received by the young drivers. Only one out of a sample of the young drivers interviewed felt that the parents' interventions were intrusive. Some of the youngsters were very positive about the program, underscoring the feeling of security they experienced from the parents' positive involvement.

Appendix: Agreement with the Young Driver

Signing of the contract should take place before the young driver embarks on his first solo drive.

I, (the young driver) _____, commit myself to abide by the traffic laws and to uphold the following conditions:

1. To plan the course of my drive before leaving.
2. To inform my parents about my destination, with whom I'm driving and at what time I'm coming back.
3. When I go out at night, to send two short text messages to my parents: one upon arrival at my destination and one before midnight.

We the parents, _____, commit ourselves to the following conditions:

1. To enable our son to gain as much driving experience as possible, if he fulfills his obligations.
2. To make our comments respectfully, and to view him as a full member of the community of drivers in the family.

Notes

1. As the present project focused on male young drivers, we use the male form of the pronoun to designate him throughout the chapter.
2. A suggestion for such an agreement is appended at the end of this chapter.
3. This project was conducted in cooperation with Or Yarok—The Israel Association for Prevention of Road Accidents.

References

Curry, A. E., Mirman, J. H., Kallan, M. J., Winston, F. K. & Durbin, D. R. (2012). Peer passengers: How do they affect teen crashes?. *Journal of Adolescent Health*, *50*(6), 588–594.

Glendon, A. I. (2014). An approach to novice driver training. *European Journal of Applied Psychology*, *64*, 111–122.

Guttman, N. (2012). "My son is reliable": Young drivers' parents' optimism and views on the norms of parental involvement in youth driving. *Journal of Adolescent Research*, 28(2), 241–268..

Lavi-Levavi, I., Shachar, I. & Omer, H. (2013). Training in non-violent resistance for parents of violent children: Differences between fathers and mothers. *Journal of Systemic Therapies*, *32*, 79–93.

Lotan, T. & Toledo, T. (2007). Driving patterns of young drivers within a graduated driver licensing system. Preprints of the Transportation Research Board 86th Annual Meeting (No. 07-1080).

Patton, G. C., Coffey, C., Sawyer, S. M., Viner, R. M., Haller, D. M., Bose, K., Vos, T., Ferguson, J. & Mathers, C. D. (2009). Global patterns of mortality in young people: A systematic analysis of population health data. *Lancet*, *374*(9693), 881–892.

Shimshoni, Y., Farah, H., Lotan, T., Grimberg, E., Dritter, O., Musicant, O., Toledo, T. & Omer, H. (2015). Effects of parental vigilant care and feedback on novice driver risk. *Journal of Adolescence*, *38*, 69–80.

Simons-Morton, B. G., Ouimet, M. C., Zhang, Z., Lee, S. L., Klauer, S. E., Wang, J., Chen, R., Albert, P. E. & Dingus, T. A. (2011). Crash and risky driving involvement among novice adolescent drivers and their parents. *American Journal of Public Health*, *101*, 2362–2367.

Road Safety Performance Index: Reducing road deaths among young people aged 15 to 30, 2011. http://www.etsc.eu/documents/PIN_Flash_21.PDF.

Williams, A. F., Tefft, B. C. & Grabowski, J. G. (2012). Graduated driver licensing research, 2010–present. *Journal of Safety Research*, *43*(3), 195–203.

Williams, A. F. (2003). Teenage drivers: Patterns of risk. *Journal of Safety Research*, *34*(1), 5–15.

Conclusion

Haim Omer

The different areas described above do not exhaust the fields of vigilant care. School, sexuality and eating habits are examples of additional life areas to which parents have to be attentive, initiate talks, keep an ear to the ground and take protective steps in case of need. Actually, vigilant care is broader than the sum of the fields in which it is exercised. Parents who manifest vigilant care are better able to detect new potential areas of risk and intervene effectively when warnings appear. Moreover, a child who is used to experiencing the parents' accompaniment will probably feel it whenever she is exposed to new dangers and temptations.

Until when should the parents continue to watch over their children? Our study on teen driving shows that the parents' function and influence may not be over when the child turns 18. Of course, the conditions in which they exercise their care changes as the child grows. However, even adult children may require firm measures of vigilant care in special situations—for instance, when they get into financial trouble and pressure their parents to cover their debts, or when they threaten to commit suicide (Omer & Dolberger, 2015).

In his autobiographical book *Promise at Dawn*, the French author and diplomat Roman Gary describes his special relationship with his mother, who had inculcated in him a spirit of heroic self-reliance, while at the same time maintaining intense emotional ties with him. In World War II, Gary fought as a pilot in the Air Force of Free France that operated from England. By highly convoluted maneuvers, his mother succeeded in sending him letters from her hiding place (the mother was Jewish). Those letters turned into Gary's chief emotional prop, helping him through his hardest hours. When he was wounded in battle and hovered between life and death in a military hospital, he would use his moments of consciousness to reread her letters, looking for those lines in which she instilled in him her fighting spirit. Those intimate messages helped him survive and resume fighting duty. The letter flow did not stop until the end of the war. Gary felt that his mother's letters were somehow keeping him alive. When France was liberated, he immediately traveled to meet with her. Upon arriving at the village in which she had been hiding, he was shocked to discover that she had been dead for a year. When she understood her end was near, she had decided she would write a series of letters postdated to the coming months, and have them sent to him, one at a time. She felt her son would need her voice in his difficult moments. She thus decided to continue watching over him from beyond her grave.

Reference

Omer, H. & Dolberger, D. I. (2015). Helping parents cope with suicide threats: An approach based on non-violent resistance. *Family Process*, *10*, 1–17.

List of Contributors

Tal Carty, The Inter-Disciplinary Center, Herzlya, Israel

Oren Dritter, PhD, Clinical Psychologist, in private practice

Yoel Everett, BA, IDC (Interdisciplinary Center) Herzliah

Tal Fisher, Non-Violent Resistance School, Israel

Gabriela Hanga, Tel-Aviv University, Israel

Avigail Hirsch-Asa, MA, Clinical Psychologist, in private practice

Israeli Juvenile Probation Service, Israel

C. T. Juravel, MA, Clinical Psychologist, in private practice

Zohar Lotringer, Tel-Aviv University, Israel

Yael Nevat, MA, Financial Consultant, in private practice

Haim Omer, Tel-Aviv University, Israel

Or Yarok Association for Prevention of Road Accidents, Israel

Yael Rothman-Kabir, Tel-Aviv University, Israel

Shai Satran, Hebrew University of Jerusalem, Israel

Yaron Sela, Tel-Aviv University, Israel

Y. Shimshoni, Tel-Aviv University, Israel

Dan Solomon, MA, Clinical Psychologist, in private practice

Index

adult children 138
alcohol *see* cigarettes, alcohol and drugs
allowance, discussions about 91–3
anchoring function 19–21, 48
anti-social behavior, predictors of 8
anxious vigilance 18
authority 20, 104; authoritarian parenting style 11, 98; authoritative stance 21

behavioral control 4–5

child resistance 46–61; child's social reality 56; confrontation and disconnection 47; coping scenario 60; decisiveness, conveying 49–51; expectations of immediate change 46; help-seeking parent 53; how parents can strengthen their position 48; managing confrontations 48–9; parental strength 49; parents capitulating 50; persistent vigilant care 46–7; running away, threat of 53–7; suicide threats 57–60; support network 51–3; threats, preparing to deal with 51; ultimatum 47
cigarettes, alcohol and drugs 98–107; child's lack of respect 102; 'dependence' 103; parents' self-control 104; preparatory talk 98, 103; quasi-formal talk 100; rites of passage 98; smokers, parents who are 100; talk's success 99
computers and the internet 108–17; child's commitment 112; commercial risk 108; contact risk 108; content risk 108; disconnection of internet 114; Facebook 110; parental commitment 112; parents' dilemma 108; pornography 111; preparatory conversation 109; Problematic Internet Use 108; project 115–16; risk, categories of 108; risk domains 110–11; surplus formality 110; virtual world 109, 114; written announcement 113

daily life, vigilant care in 31–45; accessibility, openness and self-control 40–2; conveying messages without arousing resistance 42–4; cooperation between parents 35–7; family activities 31; family friends 38; grandparents 37; joint scenarios, building of 44; network of vigilant care 33–4; open dialogue 41; privacy reflex 34; problematic poles (preacher and friend) 39; restorative justice 34; routine contact 31–3; school personnel 38; support from outside the nuclear family 37–8; talking with the child 39
decisiveness, conveying 49–51
delay, principle of 131
diabetes 118–23; counselor 118; diabetes' talks 121; empathic expression 121; family conflict 118; family routine 119; formal announcement 120; "ping-pong interactions" 119; planned text messages 121; preventing escalation 120; project 122–3; reminders 121; supporters 120; treatment regimen, adherence to 118
disclosure: description 7; disrespect and 34; friend's 111; intimate 42; parental 52; spontaneous 7–8
driving *see* teen driving
drugs *see* cigarettes, alcohol and drugs

Facebook 110–11
family activities 31
financial behavior *see* money
focused attention 15–16
fragmentation, crisis of 9–10
friends 73–85; child's inner voices 82–3; illusion of control 78; involving friends and relatives 78–9; loyalty, misplaced 80; open attention 76; peer group, attraction to 75; privacy reflex 77; respect and resistance 79–80; risk, kinds of 73; telephone round 80–2; unilateral action 76; virtual world 73; who my children's friends are 76–8

Gary, R. 138
good enough mother 67
grandparents 37

helicopter parenting 3

inner voices, child's 82–3
internet *see* computers and the internet
Israeli Juvenile Probation Service 126
IVDR (in-vehicle data recorder) appliance 135

joint scenarios, building of 44
juvenile offenders, vigilant care among 124–9; age range 124; announcement delivery 125; interventions, parental drop-out rates 124; open attention 126; preventing escalation 125; project 125–7; safety net, support network as 126; short-term group training 125; source of legitimacy 126; traffic light metaphor 125; "treatment as usual" 126

Kerr, M. 6, 9

lies 62–72; abandonment 66; attempt to prove to the child that he is lying 64–5; children's rating of lies 63; cognitive achievement 62; developmental consequences of lying 63–4; evidence 65; good enough mother 67; habitual lying 65; intensifying vigilant care 65–7; interpersonal and disciplinary consequences of lying 67–71; lies that hurt others 71; mentalization 62; mother–daughter bond, deterioration of 64; siblings, conflicts between 66;
transparency, creating 69; trust or no trust 66; violations of trust 68
loyalty 79; misplaced 80; peer group 64

mentalization 62
money 86–97; allowance, discussions about 91–3; examples from conversations 88; harmful financial behavior 93–6; mental reality 89; plan for the "money talk" 86; transparency, creation of 95; withstanding the child's inappropriate demands 90–1
"monitoring knowledge" 10
mother–daughter bond, deterioration of 64

network of vigilant care 33–4
new authority *see* daily life, vigilant care in
non-violent resistance 6, 14

open attention 11, 14, 76, 126
overparenting 2–4

parental knowledge 6–7, 32, 118
parental monitoring 1, 21; components 8; developmental risks and 4; risk and 2
parental presence 13–14, 21; building joint scenarios 44; cooperation between parents 37; contacting the child's friends 56, 77, 81; diabetes and 119; driving and 130, 132–3; internet and 110; juvenile offenders and 125; money and 86, 91; resistance to 43, 50; routine contact 32; trust 65
parental self-control 48
parents, cooperation between 35–7
peer group, attraction to 75
"ping-pong interactions" 119
pornography 111
principle of delay 131
privacy reflex 17, 34, 77
Problematic Internet Use (PIU) 108; *see also* computers and the internet
protective action 16
psychological control 4–5

resistance *see* child resistance
restorative justice 34
running away, threat of 53–7

safe haven 20
school personnel 38

self-determination theory 5–6
siblings, conflicts between 66
social domain 5–6
spying 18–19
Stattin, H. 6, 9
suicide threats 57–60

teen driving 130–7; accompanied-driving period 131; agreement with the young driver 136; "drivers' talks" 131–3; IVDR appliance 135; licensing process 130; limiting driving rights 134–5; principle of delay 131; project 135–6; risks 130; text messages 133; transition to 'solo' driving 132–4; warning signals 133
telephone round 80–2
text messages, planned 121
threats, preparing to deal with 51
traffic light metaphor 125
transparency, creating 69, 95
"treatment as usual" (TAU) 126
trust 16; alarm signs and 12; dichotomy 66; unconditional 18; violations of 67–8

unconditional trust, trap of 18
unilateral action 76

vigilant care 1–30; anchoring function 19–21; anxious vigilance 18; calls for integration 10–11; cumulative effects of critique 7–9; dilemma 1; disclosure 7; focused attention 15–16; fragmentation, crisis of 9–10; "monitoring knowledge" 10; non-violent resistance 6; open attention 11, 14–15; overparenting 2–4; parental knowledge 6–7; parental monitoring 1; parental presence 13; privacy reflex 17; privacy, trust and spying 16–19; programs of vigilant care 14; protective action 16; psychological and behavioral control 4–5; safe haven 20; shift in cultural norms 2; social domain and self-determination theory 5–6; spying trap 19; training effects 9; unconditional trust, trap of 18
virtual world 73, 109, 114

Winnicott, D. 67

For Product Safety Concerns and Information please contact our EU
representative GPSR@taylorandfrancis.com
Taylor & Francis Verlag GmbH, Kaufingerstraße 24, 80331 München, Germany

www.ingramcontent.com/pod-product-compliance
Lightning Source LLC
Chambersburg PA
CBHW051615230426
43668CB00013B/2118